OF FAITH IN A CULTURE OF CHANGE

LEARNING TO CREATE A COMMUNITY

the out of bounds

Church?

D0170367

www.emergentys.com

emergent
ys

ZONDERVAN

STEVE TAYLOR

Youth Specialties Products, 300 South Pierce Street, El Cajon, CA 92020 are published by
Zondervan, 5300 Patterson Avenue Southeast, Grand Rapids, MI 49530.

Library of Congress Cataloging-in-Publication Data

Taylor, Steve, 1968-
  The out of bounds church : learning to create a community of faith in
a culture of change / by Steve Taylor.
    p. cm.
  ISBN 0-310-25904-5 (pbk.)
  1. Christianity and culture. 2. Popular culture--Religious
aspects--Christianity. 3. Missions. I. Title.
  BR115.C8T395 2005
  261--dc22

#56721998   2004023731

Web site addresses listed in this book were current at the time of publication. Please contact
Youth Specialties via e-mail (YS@YouthSpecialties.com) to report URLs that are no longer
operational and replacement URLs if available.

Editorial direction by Carla Barnhill
Art direction by Jay Howver
Proofreading by Joanne Heim and Laura Gross
Cover design by Rule 29
Interior design by Holly Sharp

Printed in the United States

05 06 07 08 09 10 / / 9 8 7 6 5 4 3 2

This book is for those who
dream the dream
of finding God in the desert of
the [postmodern] real.

Making our own direction
but we will never forget our connection.
Always stick to your roots with you
Whenever you're down remember your crew.
Don't you fall from grace [my friend]
be cool with your space
check your pace, it ain't a race[1.]

Contents

foreword by Olive fleming Drane and John Drane

As I opened the first postcard, I found myself thinking that Karl Barth used to talk about having a Bible in one hand and a newspaper in the other, only to find Steve then said this a couple of pages later.   In fact I found this on a number of occasions, which is one reason why I think many readers will find their own half-formed thoughts articulated for them in the following pages, putting into words what they intuitively know.

Perhaps that in itself is all that needs to be said by way of introducing this book. It certainly identifies it as a volume that can speak to the hearts of today's post-modern people in ways that more propositional forms of theology increasingly fail to do. Steve's account of his own journey is strongly grounded in the stories of real life, interrogated in the light of the historic Christian tradition—a process which leads to much creative theological reflection, and inevitably connects with the life experience of those many others all around the world who today are embarked upon similar spiritual journeys.

The heart of this book focuses on a need to find new ways of expressing and celebrating Christian faith in a world that is increasingly interested in spiritual meaning, whether that is demonstrated in the search for life-giving ways of nourishing our own lives, or as a concern about the apparently destructive capabilities of spiritual fanaticism. It will speak to all who share these concerns, and do so in innovative ways that draw us deeper into the gospel story, and consequently, closer to Christ.

Olive Fleming Drane
John Drane

Foreword by Doug McConnell

On the banks of a river winding its way through the jungle, a family gathered to meet the new headmaster of the mission school. As the man stepped out of the canoe, the older of the missionary family's children welcomed the teacher with an invitation to explore this isolated world through the eyes of an 8-year-old. There were few choices, but plenty of time to make them. Like the earliest missionaries to the tribal worlds of the globe, this family lived among the people as faithful gospel witnesses.

This book includes the same two people nearly 30 years later. Steve Taylor was that young student, and I was that young teacher. There was something about the curiosity of Steve's approach to life even then that was more instructive than most. Now I stand next to him and observe the world through his eyes once again. In contrast, the time is short, but the choices are plentiful. As we embark on the global missional response, there are lessons we can take from the careful engagement of previous generations of Christian witness.

In this book Steve expands our growing understanding of faith as it must be lived out in the world impacted by postmodernity. Advancing the discussion of the emergent church, he adds perspective by identifying the dimensions of theological reflection in order to capture birth images, creative play, spiritual tourism, redemptive portals, and missional interweaving. Along with these fascinating discussions, Taylor adds new roles for the church to consider such as, midwives, chefs, tour guides, cybermonks, and DJs. Knowing the love affair globalization has with new stuff, one can only imagine the clothing and logos that will accompany these emerging church ministers.

One of the great strengths of Steve's contribution comes out of his insistence on "extreme discipleship" rather than "Christianity lite." A concept that has permeated missiological reflection for the past three decades is contextualization. Put simply, it is the witness of the gospel in and through local contexts so as to answer the heart questions of people where they are in life. Instead of rigorously copying the forms and answers of a different time and place, missional engagement seeks to share the gospel in such a way that new communities of believers are born of the soil of their time and place. What has been difficult for traditional missions and churches to grasp is the collapse of space and time in the postmodern context.

Taylor joins a growing group of missiologists who are grappling with the realities, both virtual and historical, of the emerging church. Reading this book collapsed three decades for me. I remember the vibrancy of my early missionary years filled with bright students like Steve Taylor. The world retains many little villages along the banks of jungle rivers, yet it has added many new villages along the streams of cyberspace. If we are to remain faithful to the gospel, we must explore new forms of missional interweaving in all the cultures of the world. This is a book for missional explorers.

Doug McConnell
Dean, School of Intercultural Studies
Fuller Theological Seminary

Introduction

It is time to listen carefully. Can you hear the grind and groan as the tectonic plates of our culture shift? We live on the fault lines of a widespread cultural change. Institutions are in decline. Ancient spiritualities have re-emerged. World music has collided with pop music. The center looks out to the edge.

In the midst of all this change, innovative expressions of church and worship are emerging across the globe. New approaches to creativity, community, and ritual are being practiced in small towns and urban centers. There is a fresh understanding of what the church can be in the midst of this tension between the old and the new. Based on my postgraduate research, my networks of friends around the world, and my experiences as a community builder within the emerging church, this book is my effort to uncover the practices and theologies of Christian groups surfing the postmodern mission edges.

Think of this book as postcards from the emerging church. These postcards include themes of birth, creative play, spiritual tourism, community, missional interface, and DJ sampling. The book weaves the life and liturgy of emergent Christian groups with biblical reflection and the riches of the Christian tradition, all in dialogue with the practices of contemporary culture.

A brief note about the format of the book

A postcard—picture on front and words on back—introduces each chapter. Each postcard is written from a different place around the globe and together they form the story of a world journey. Each postcard is followed by a chapter exploring the questions posed by the postcard and each emerging church situation. You will also find a list of related websites and books at the end of each chapter. Since websites do change, I will keep an updated list on my weblog: www.emergentkiwi.org.nz.

The postcards tell of a trip —in life, in mission, in emerging church planting. And each postcard explores a question:

- How could the notion of birth and midwifery apply to the emerging church?
- What is the place of creativity in the emerging church and the implications for our spirituality in a highly visual world?

- What is incarnational mission in a world that's online 24/7?
- What is the importance of community in the emerging church?
- How can the emerging church interface community and mission?
- How is the emerging church DJ-ing gospel and culture, mixing image and sound, ancient and future, to create a remix for a new world?

You can read this book much like a magazine, browsing each postcard as it catches your eye. You can read either down or across. If you read down, you will strike a more ordered, coherent textual reflection. If you read across, you will find a less structured grouping of material: music you could play while you read a particular section, visual material, spiritual rituals, quotes, websites, practices from the emerging church, and comments from various voices.

You can also read the thoughts of other voices. I invited a number of people to comment on the book, people from Scotland to Sydney, from Chicago to Cambridge, from mature friends to new Christians, from practitioners to reflectors. Their instructions were to "to disagree, to provide an example, to add a prayer or a ritual, to provide another perspective."

Maggi Dawn is chaplain of Robinson College, Cambridge, UK. She was a professional musician and singer and has been involved in developing alternative and new forms of worship since 1990 (her last CD is *Elements*). Maggi holds an MA and PhD in theology, both from Cambridge University, where she continues to teach and supervise theology students. She has written chapters in *The Post-Evangelical Debate, Anglicanism:The Answer to Modernity?* and *The Rite Stuff*.

Olive and John Drane are both active practitioners and educators. Olive is the author of *Clowns, Storytellers, Disciples* and has a worldwide ministry in theology and the creative arts. She is a mission consultant for the Baptist Union of Scotland and is also an adjunct professor of practical theology at Fuller Theological Seminary (California). She is joint author (with John) of *Family Fortunes: Faith-full Caring for Today's Families*.

John is author of *The McDonaldization of the Church* and has taught at Stirling and Aberdeen Universities in Scotland, Fuller Seminary, and other institutions around the world. He is co-chair of the Mission Theology Advisory Group of the Archbishops' Council of the Church of England and of Churches Together in Britain and Ireland.

Andrew Jones is a global networker among the emerging church. With a nose for the fresh currents of God, he has RV-ed around the United States, lived in Prague, and now rents in London. He blogs at tallskinnykiwi.typepad.com.

Gerard Kelly lives between France and the UK. He is a speaker and poet. He has written *Retrofuture* and a range of books for Spring Harvest. His passion is leadership development and the unchurched in Europe, expressed through the Bless Network, an agency fostering mission innovation in Europe. He loves cigars and curries.

Cathy Kirkpatrick is a Sydney-based digital designer. She was a founding member of Cafe Church in Glebe, a suburb of Sydney, and had a hand in *The Prodigal Project*. Now she keeps tropical fish, cooks a lot of spicy food, and grinds beans in honor of good friends.

Sally Morgenthaler lives in Colarado and is a well-known worship consultant, author, and speaker. She wrote *Worship Evangelism: Inviting Unbelievers into the Presence of God* and founded Sacramentis.com. Sally is also president of Digital Glass Productions, a new genre of worship videos for the emerging church. She has worked as the on-site worship design consultant for Pathways Church in Denver, and as adjunct professor of worship at both Denver Seminary and Covenant Bible College.

Mark Pierson is founding pastor of Cityside Baptist Church in Auckland, New Zealand. He is also co-author of *The Prodigal Project* and *Fractals for Worship: Alternative Resources for the Emerging Church* CD-ROM.

Kelli Robson is a surprised Christian. She grew up going to church with her parents because that's what people did. As a preteen, she stopped feeling like she fit in that box. By the age of 25 she was sure atheism was the truth, until God made her unsure. She was recently baptized at a quiet beach in Auckland, New Zealand, with friends and our church family from Graceway. She was raised in Kansas but lives permanently in New Zealand. She is an editor and a "mad-keen" soccer player.

Robert Webber is referred to as one of the real and practical experts in the "art of Christian worship." Robert is an author of more than 40 books on the subject of worship and spirituality, and is a popular conference and workshop communicator. He is on the faculty of Northern Baptist Seminary in the suburbs of Chicago where he serves as director of the MA in worship and spirituality program and teaches courses in the DMin in worship studies. He is also the president of the Institute for Worship Studies, which offers advanced degrees in worship studies.

Part One Culture Shapers

Part One
Culture Shapers

HI FROM AUCKLAND, NEW ZEALAND.
I'M STEVE.

A FEW YEARS AGO MY FRIENDS--ACTIVE, THOUGHTFUL, CREATIVE 20-SOMETHINGS-- WERE, IN THE WORDS OF REM, LOSING THEIR RELIGION. TOGETHER WE CREATED A COMMUNAL SPACE, GRACEWAY, THAT MIGHT NOURISH OUR CHRISTIAN FAITH.

IT WAS THEN THAT I HEARD THE TERM "EMERGING CHURCH." I SET OUT TO COMPARE NOTES, COLLECTING STORIES IN UK CAFES AND TRAIN STATIONS, EXPERIENCING THE EMERGING CHURCH FROM SEATTLE TO SYDNEY. I COMPLETED A PhD, CRITICALLY REFLECTING ON MY EXPERIENCES AND THESE STORIES.

THIS BOOK RECORDS THE POSTCARDS OF MY JOURNEY THROUGH THE EMERGING EDGE. IT'S A JOURNEY THAT HAS ENRICHED MY FAITH AND MY LIFE. I HOPE IT DOES THE SAME FOR YOU.

2882

Post Card

THIS SPACE FOR ADDRESS ONLY

1—

Postcard 1:
Beyond Romeo and Juliet

I sit on the fault lines of a cultural shift. In my right hand, I hold a video remote. In my left hand, I hold the gospel of Jesus. I am born for such a time as this. So are you. Ours is the task of communicating this gospel in an age of change. Ours is the task of following Jesus into the future of this cultural shift.

Last century, Karl Barth wrote that the task of Christian communication was to sit with the newspaper in one hand and the Bible in the other. Last century. That was when "gay" meant happy and the Berlin Wall marked East from West. Last century. That was before multi-media, the Internet, and virtual reality. Jesus and the Bible have not changed—both have captured my heart. But the world I sit in looks totally different than it did even ten years ago. The future of faith looks increasingly fragile.

Press PLAY

In 1968, the year I was born, Franco Zeffarelli produced a film version of *Romeo and Juliet*. Zeffarelli realized that while Shakespeare's ancient text had not changed, the people reading the text were totally different. It was time to focus on historical literature through the lens of a contemporary context.

The 60-second cinematic introduction to Zeffarelli's *Romeo and Juliet* is one long, slow, camera pan. From a distance, the lens casts its gaze languorously over a city. The viewer is allowed a detached distance from the affairs and passions of that city. A lone male voice speaks over a soft, orchestral lilt. Slowly a horse and cart emerge from an ancient city gate and clip their way across the screen.

fault lines of a cultural shift: I like the image of cultural eras as tectonic plates—they're usually quiet below the surface. We don't necessarily notice that they're holding up our society every day. Then they start moving, and the effects are dramatic. The culture has moved under society's feet, under the church's foundations. We're in a whole new place, from the ground up and even deeper.
—Kelli Robson

on the big screen: *Romeo and Juliet,* directed by Franco Zeffarelli, Paramount Studio, 1968.

on the big screen: *William Shakespeare's Romeo and Juliet,* directed by Baz Luhrmann, Fox Home Entertainment, 1996.

Rush ahead to 1996, less than 30 years later, to Baz Luhrmann's cinematic version of *Romeo and Juliet*. Luhrmann, too, realized that while the ancient text had not changed, the audience had. Once again it was time to mix the old with the new.

Luhrmann's *Romeo and Juliet* is set in Verona Beach, a modern city of guns, money, and greed. The 125-second cinematic introduction starts with static and channel surfing—welcome to the world of multi-media. A TV appears center screen and the news announcer, a black female, speaks—welcome to the celebration of the ethnic and the edge. The camera zooms the detached viewer into the TV and plunges down two lines of apartment blocks—welcome to a shift from objectivity to immersion. Text and image are mixed with an explosive soundtrack. Images flash by: a statue of Jesus, city scenes, helicopters, advertising, police around a body, newspaper headlines. Flames engulf a newspaper—both image and text—telling of the Capulets and Montagues—welcome to ancient text amid a cultural shift.

Two directors, two movies, two cultures, one text. Both movies tell a story that has been told (and contextualized) for centuries. Yet in these two versions of the same story, there exist cues about the times in which—for which—they were made. Not just the trappings of the culture, mind you, but its very essence.

Culture is like the air we breathe. Without it we would die. It lies all around us, unrecognized and unmentioned. And then, every now and again, air becomes a talking point—when my city has a pollution warning, when I am forced to study air at the university level, when my breath clouds in deep white billows in front of my face on an icy morning. Then I think about air. In the same way, the culture shifts between Zeffarelli's era and Lurhmann's have come so subtly that we may not necessarily notice them until some director pops them up on a movie screen in such an extraordinary way that we can no longer ignore them.

When I think about the cultural "air" in which Luhrmann contemporizes *Romeo and Juliet*, I find four clear marks of the postmodern culture: fragmentation of fast/cutting, individual pick-and-mix lifestyles, tribalism, and the ethnic edge.

Fast/cutting and fragmentation

Fast/cutting is a filmmaking term for the rapid cutting between one image and the next. Fast/cutting is the mainstay of much contemporary video communication. It is a feature of Luhrmann's introduction of *Romeo and Juliet*—a montage of city scenes, people rioting, and images of Jesus. Graphics and text flash by, juxtaposed and fleeting.

Fast/cutting also shows up in the use of sound bites in the news. Studies show that the average length of a sound bite has decreased from 40 seconds in 1968, to 8 seconds in 1996.[2] The way in which we are given information has changed, and therefore the process of thinking about that information has changed. In every way, we have moved from Zeffarelli's slow single-shot pan to Luhrmann's rapidly moving juxtaposition of text, sound, and image.

I often show the introductions to these two versions of *Romeo and Juliet* to groups wanting to explore cultural change. After we watch the introductions, I have the groups list the changes, not just in the filming techniques but in the aspects of the culture that these techniques represent.

After doing this with a range of mainstream churches, I did it with an emerging church group. Halfway through the exercise, a voice spoke up. "It's real. Luhrmann's one. It's got more content." This comment reminded me that technology influences, even changes, the way we think. When you spend your life immersed in the fast/cutting of text and image, fast/cutting becomes the way you process and learn. Suddenly, the slow camera pan and the monologue become artificial, false, hard to follow. When you're used to surfing from image to image, three point sermons start to sound like archaic King James English.

time bites: Fast/cutting is a fundamental part of my framework. I live in shorter bites than my mother. I work in shorter bites, rest in shorter bites, speak in shorter bites, think in shorter bites, so sometimes I find myself offering God short bites. I set aside an hour to think quietly, pray, meditate and my brain jumps. Is it better to fight for focus, or let the flux of bites flow up to God? I think it's important to offer God stillness in my mind, to be still and know that he is God. For me, nature has proven to be the best way to slow my thoughts and reflect on who God is, eternally, apart from the flux of human fragments around me.
—Kelli Robson

Fast/cutting is a surface technology. It demonstrates a change in the way culture communicates. But fast/cutting is also like the leaves of a tree—just as leaves are nourished by underground roots, so fast/cutting is nourished by underground ideas. It isn't just our understanding of our culture that has become fragmented, but the culture itself.

In his book, *The Postmodern Condition*, French thinker Jean François Lyotard investigates the ways in which computer technologies influence people's thinking. His findings lead him to argue for "incredulity toward metanarratives."[3] In other words, over time and with the help of our tech-centered world, we have grown to distrust the idea of one overarching story that can be used to make sense of everything. Our thinking has fragmented into many privatized stories.

And that brings with it a whole new set of questions. As Morpheus uses the remote to change landscapes around Neo in *The Matrix,* the question is, "Which reality is the real one?" As war is constructed in *Wag the Dog,* the question is, "Who controls reality?" As Forrest Gump is digitally inserted into the black-and-white archives of U.S. history, the question is, "What is true history?" As Bono from U2 sings, "Even better than the real thing," the question is, "Where are you standing to view reality?"

These movies, these cultural leaves, emerge from underground thinking. Back in 1972, French thinker Michel Foucault argued, "Truth is a thing of this world; it is produced only by multiple forms of constraint."[4]

Consider the work of Jacques Derrida, the father of deconstructionism. I used to think of his work as part of the remote world of academia—until he packed out one of the largest auditoriums in my city. I might have considered him elitist, but my city obviously considered him inspirational. In an article titled, "Des Tours de Babel," Derrida explodes previously universal and objective ways of viewing faith and language.

He argues that at the tower of Babel we see the emergence of the "city where understanding is no longer

on the big screen:
The Matrix, directed by Larry and Andy Wachowski, Warner Studios, 1999; *Wag the Dog,* directed by Barry Levinson, New Line Studios, 1997; *Forrest Gump,* directed by Robert Zemeckis, Paramount Studios, 1994.

in the CD player:
U2, "Even Better than the Real Thing," *Achtung Baby,* Uni/Island, 1992.

possible."[5] Rather than unify, language confuses, separates, and fragments. Subversively, Derrida pushes us further. He uses ancient languages to argue that God's name is Babel. Rather than unify, God divides, fragments, or, to use Derrida's favorite term, God deconstructs.[6] It is not the task of this book to respond to Derrida.[7] Rather, I want to point out that a packed town hall listened to Derrida deconstruct Western ways of looking at reality. The universality of language, philosophy, rationality, even religion, has become unstable and subjective. This fragmenting approach has been cleverly called, not deduction or induction, but *unduction*, the reversal of all attempts to achieve knowledge and truth.[8] Such fragmentation, whether at the surface or on underground levels, can result in contemporary cultures being both pessimistic and playfully pluralistic.

Modernity's dream of a better, brighter future is replaced by kind of hopelessness. "It's dark in there—in the Future I mean. It's not a good place . . . I feel like sleeping for a thousand years—that way I'll never have to be around for this weird new future," writes a disillusioned young adult in a Douglas Coupland novel.[9] In Coupland's *Polaroids from the Dead*, a hippie mother puts her children to bed while telling them the story of the skeleton that enters the gleaming modern city.[10] The city is in a drought. Its creative visionaries die. The skeleton speaks, urging the dying city to pray for a vision of the afterlife. It's a poignant moment of pessimism that serves to contrast the idealism of hippie dreams with a dying, prayerless city.

The notion of postmodern pluralism, the fast/cutting approach to life, needs to be applied with care. Pluralism is not new; modern liberalism prized plurality. However, that brand of pluralism remained private. Plural beliefs were welcomed, as long as they lay within the overarching, universal metanarrative of the Western dream.

In contrast, a postmodern pluralism celebrates the breaking apart of the metanarrative. Instead of one public, tolerant answer to the big questions, we now have

on the bookshelf: John Caputo, *The Prayers and Tears of Jacques Derrida. Religion Without Religion.* Bloomington & Indianapolis: Indiana University Press, 1997.

on the bedside table: Douglas Coupland, "How Clear is Your Vision of Heaven?" *Polaroids from the Dead,* Regan: New York, 1996, 55-63.

eight kinds of coffee:
Espresso
Cappuccino
Turkish Coffee
Cafetière/French Press
Vacuum Post
Drip Filter
Cold Press
Percolator

competing answers—a mosaic of perspectives and ideas and beliefs. We stand at the postmodern coffee counter, individually choosing our own mix of worldviews—one shot or two, small or grande, milk or soy. The public worldview selection list goes on. We have little choice but to move from image to image, idea to idea, with the speed and vigor of Luhrmann's opening montage.

Pick-and-mix lifestyles

Fragmentation represents both crisis and opportunity. In Luhrmann's world, the camera zooms into a city where multiple communities are visible. Such communities are evident in the gender and ethnicity of the black, female newsreader and the black, male chief of police breaking up scenes of rioting between various groups, as well as in the juxtaposition of the Montague and Capulet families. As our culture liquifies into a montage of choices, the range of lifestyle options becomes evident. Identity is constructed from the pick-and-mix options available within the multifaceted culture.

The term *liquid modernity* has been used to describe the cultural shift from the solid, production-oriented, structured confines of modernity to an insecure, individual-driven, flexible way of living in contemporary society. The shift in the culture and the ways in which those shifts change the people living in the culture becomes an ongoing dance where each partner leads for a time.

As those of us living in a postmodern world negotiate our way through a piecemeal society, our assumptions about our place in that society are subtly altered. Angela McRobbie notes, "The reason why postmodernism appeals to a wide number of young people is that they themselves are experiencing the enforced fragmentation of impermanent work and low career opportunities."[11] There is little that is permanent here—not your job, not your home, not your family or your friends. It is the age of the cell phone, the laptop, and the PDA, where the hot desk has replaced the office desk and the satellite has replaced the landline. While the factory prized production, routine, and teamwork, postmodern industry values speed, innovation, and independence.

The Internet may be the ultimate in pick-and-mix living. Individuals are freed from external institutions, whether they are religious, familial, or business. The individual Web surfer clicks and browses. A virtual screen offers a global world of possibilities to each individual mouse. The surfer can construct his or her identity in a world of chat and e-groups. The Internet never sleeps as all these equal websites, bound together by the egalitarian hyperlink, offer their graphics and text. This is a world of individualized meaning, in which the consumer clicks supreme.

At the heart of this individual pick-and-mix is a search for identity. Sociologists Madan Sarup and Tasneem Raja note, "Millions of people in the world today are searching for 'roots': they go back to the town, the country, or the continent they came from long ago . . . identity is a construction."[12] Nowhere is this more evident than at the mall.

Identity and lifestyle walk hand-in-hand through the malls that define contemporary culture. At the mall you can survey the wide range of identity garments—the hip, the classic, the bold, the subdued, the sweet, the sexy. It is at the mall that we see the extent to which "product image and style and design take over from modern metanarratives the task of conferring meaning."[13] It is at the mall that you pick and mix your lifestyle. At the same time, the selection isn't as individualized as it sounds. The choices are still pre-selected by powers outside of our control.

Even in the seemingly endless sea of choices, the pessimism of postmodernity bobs to the surface: "I am a 16-year-old girl and I attend a public high school in downtown Colorado Springs. Since childhood my body has been a billboard. Before I could read there were labels on my shoes, on my jeans, and across my bosom."[14]

Identity is not just about clothes. It's also about the consumption of experiences in an experience-driven

in the CD player: "My Culture," *1 Giant Leap*, Palm Pictures, 2001. This is a song about the bittersweet experience of the richness of ancestral identity tempered by the lack of father love. How do we reweave identity in a culture of broken relationships?

on the big screen: I love the scene in *Whale Rider* when the granddaughter questions her grandfather about their family origins. The grandfather uses the rope to explain how their identity is a weaving together of many strands. The rope is then broken. How do we reweave identity in our contemporary world? *Whale Rider*, directed by Niki Caro, Columbia Tristar, 2003.

the body billboard:
As a visiting storyteller and theologian at the Reel Spirituality Conference in Hollywood in November 1999, I witnessed a young woman—I will always remember the bright green hair—having a moment of self-discovery during a discussion with movie directors. "Look at me," she said. "I'm a walking advert for the Gap. I wouldn't know who I was if I didn't have these logos." Incidentally, she went on to complain about the way she, and others, were being exploited not only by the McDonaldized culture, but by movie directors who failed to offer young people appropriate alternative role models.
—Olive Drane

economy.[15] The humble coffee bean can be grown as a commodity. It can be converted into a product. It can be sold as a service. Or it can be the center of an experience in a place that defines your identity. Experiences become another accessory the individual consumer can use to compliment a lifestyle.

Identity is also about making our life stories public; I define myself as I tell you who I am. That telling is not always a verbal exchange. Notice how widespread tattoos and body piercing are among the emerging culture. These are visual symbols of experiences, public mementos of a life lived. Ask my friends why they got a tattoo and you will hear part of their story. Ask me why I have three earrings and you'll discover that each piercing was carefully chosen to assert my identity first as a Christian and then as a minister. In many ways, body modification is the natural offspring of a culture in which identity is found in how we look and the experiences we live out.

Spirituality is another area in which contemporary culture is busy picking and mixing in a consumptive search for individual meaning. In Luhrmann's introduction, the statues of Jesus are a repeated image. The camera circles us around the outstretched hands of Jesus. Romeo, played by movie star Leonardo DiCaprio, peeks through an open door into a church. Throughout the film, candles glow and white crosses gleam. In Luhrmann's world, spirituality is a very visible lifestyle option.

Douglas Coupland has written a stream of books from within the emerging culture. Intriguingly, Coupland's characters often become spiritual, even though Coupland himself has no religious background. They go out into the wilderness and jump naked into freezing cold pools to confess, "My secret is that I need God."[16] They celebrate Christmas by creating their own experiential spirituality, lighting candles, and covering the whole house with "small moments of intense, flaring beauty"[17] that open up new ways of being family.

The very presence of contemporary spirituality is in rich contrast to the stark secularism of Zeffarelli's era. The "God is dead" movement of the 1960s toasted "what-you-see-is-what-you-get" and the triumph of rational objectivity. Yet beneath the peat of disinterest, spirituality smoldered. In the undergrowth, the creators of *Buffy the Vampire Slayer* and *The X-Files* dreamed. The spark flickers and DiCaprio opens the door to candlelit mystery.

This is both good news and bad news for the church. The good news is that spirituality has not died. The bad news is that the traditional modes of thinking about and talking about Christianity no longer appeal to those living in a changing culture. In today's pick-and-mix supermarket of spiritual options, people are not often looking for the one big story. People in the postmodern era are not interested in New Age 101 or Introduction to Buddhism any more than they are looking to grab onto the whole biblical metanarrative. Instead, they are simply sampling a meditative technique from here and a healing crystal from there.

Yet in this crisis there is opportunity. We can offer the culture the richness of our Christian heritage—the beauty of new expressions of faith and community that have the power to sustain us in a time of fragmentation.

Tribalism

As our contemporary world breaks apart, new tribes emerge. In Luhrmann's *Romeo and Juliet*, new tribes are signalled by the newsreader, the chief of police, the modern-day Montague and Capulet families, and the tribal gangs inhabiting the street scene. All of this is in stark contrast to Zeffarelli's lone tribal representative, the British-sounding male narrator. Postmodern society has been likened to an airport departure lounge. Membership is fluid, as passengers wait for the announcement of a new piece of action.[18]

But this metaphor suggests a disconnection, a sense of isolation within postmodern culture, which isn't completely accurate. In the face of this potential crisis

at home in the city: One of the most interesting new buildings in England is in the city of Manchester. "Urbis" is home to a significant exhibition of the built environment. (The United Nations predicts that 60 percent of the world population will be urban by 2030.) People like cities, and they like them for different reasons. Cities provide spaces and networks for individuals to connect. According to cliché, you can be lonely in a city. At the same time, it is often easier to create community in a city. Experiences of loneliness and fragmentation encourage people to be intentional about looking for "community." How can the emerging church look ahead instead of running to catch up? —John and Olive Drane surfing in cyberland: Please join the conversation at www.emergentkiwi.org.nz.

the cyberpub: I had the same experience a few years back when a group of friends created our own "cyberpub." This was an e-mail group that became a regular meeting place for a dozen or so friends whose actual lives, spread across three continents, made physical meetings infrequent. We found ourselves talking with an honesty and directness previously avoided—even though several of us had been friends for many years. During a significant and transitional phase of my life, the "cyberpub" was a genuine discipleship group for me and, at times, the most useful "church" I attended.
—Gerard Kelly

of fragmentation, new forms of community have begun to spring forth. As an experiment in emerging ways of community, I started my own weblog, curious to discover if I would experience more or less community in the virtual world.

The answer has undoubtedly been more. I have seen relationships flourish. I have seen resources shared. I have seen horizons expand. I have even seen people who were once strangers step into each other's lives to offer financial and emotional help in times of difficulty. True, contemporary society does split the metanarrative that we once assumed offered us connection, yet new tribes are finding new ways to attach to each other.

In our contemporary world, individuals are now choosing to come together for the purpose of finding meaning in their lives; the community has become a tool for the individual. Coupland tells of Andy, Clair, and Dag, who travel into the desert "to tell stories and to make our own lives worthwhile tales in the process."[19] Together, in a tribal community, they find purpose.

Each of Coupland's ten novels focuses on a tribe, a smaller societal group of individuals who choose to find meaning together. These tribal communities are not necessarily exclusive or anti-generational. In the conclusion of his book, *Generation X*, the main character, Andy, is injured by a bird. A mentally retarded girl notices Andy's injury and proceeds to stroke him "gently with an optimistic and healing staccato caress—it was the faith-healing gesture." Andy is then embraced by all the members of the girl's mentally retarded group of friends, "an instant family, in their adoring, healing, uncritical embrace." As a result, Andy experiences what Coupland calls a "crush of love."[20] It is a striking vision of the power of human relationships—even those between seemingly disparate people—to bring redemption.

The ethnic edge

Technology has given us unprecedented access to other tribes—voices and experiences quite removed from our own. Nelson Mandela writes of meeting a teenage Inuit in Alaska who had seen Mandela's release from imprisonment on Robben Island. "What struck me so forcefully was how small the planet had become . . . Television had shrunk the world."[21] The universality of electronic media promotes local diversity. Hence, Peter Corney comments that the "contemporary city is a culturally rich and fascinating place, but it also produces a new tribalism of subcultures. Such vast cities are tied together by one factor: the electronic media—which paradoxically both homogenizes and fragments culture."[22]

Music is another carrier of the ethnic edge. Cultural historian Steve Redhead describes how over the last 20 years the rock and pop industries have been disturbed by world music.[23] Hip-hop and similar music styles have become mainstream. Because of world music, teenagers are apt to be more connected culturally to teenagers on the other side of the world than to their parents in the next room.

On the other side of this localized diversity is global uniformity. George Ritzer observes how global corporations have used efficiency and the rationalization of "branding" to offer a homogenous and standardized product all around the world.[24] This is the global exporting of American culture, a phenomenon Ritzer calls "McDonaldization," that offers everyone everywhere the shared experience of American T-shirts, jeans, sneakers, and fast foods. Whether in China or New York, McDonalds offers a clean toilet and a Big Mac with fries. McDonalds creates an eating experience and trades on the spectacle of an image-based culture. At the same time, McDonalds responds to the edge, adding Spanish style roofs in Little Havana, Miami, and introducing the "Lomu Burger" in New Zealand, named after a local sporting star.

Ironically, the more the world is McDonaldized, the more vociferous the edge becomes and the more the edge and the center meld into one another. The media carry images of protestors who, using the globalizing tools of the Internet and airline travel, accuse global companies

the search for truth:
I don't think Gen-X spirituality is about an individualized search, but a search that's honest and genuine regarding the seeker's individual identity. Gen-Xers are seeking truth—they have just opened up the podium so that everyone has the right to share their truths and be part of defining what the truth is. We have swapped truth as defined by one individual or group for a harmonic truth defined by many voices.
—Kelli Robson

on the bedside table:
John Drane, *The McDonaldization of the Church.* London: Darton, Longman and Todd, 2000, chapter 8.

and organizations of cultural imperialism and economic exploitation. Naomi Klein's protest against globalization, *No Logo*, is now a marketing success story, carried by the technological tide of Web reference.[25] The term *glocal* has been used to describe this interplay between global and local.[26]

On the surface, the influence of the edge sounds like a very good thing. And yet there are cautions. First, beware the global underdog. While contemporary culture stretches around our globe, not all participants feel equally embraced. One dark cloud of uncertainty in this new tribalism is the shadow of fundamentalism. In a fragmented context, the simplicity of black-and-white beliefs is a powerful cocktail, one that can be intoxicating to those who find themselves disenfranchised by the powers that be. Whether Islamic, Hindu, or Christian, conservative religious communities have seen an increase in both the passion and numbers of adherents. In Luhrmann's *Romeo and Juliet*, the statues of Jesus are often placed directly between the Capulet and Montague families. The question is tantalizing: Does religion divide or unify?

Second, beware commercializing the edge. Postmodernism has been accused of celebrating the edges and margins in a manner that makes them meaningless. Postmodernism "kills everything that gives meaning and depth to the life of non-Western individuals and societies . . . When non-Western cultural artifacts appear in the West, they do so strictly as ethnic chic or empty symbols."[27] Is Western culture visiting the edge and commercializing the margins in a way that hollows out the riches of ancient and diverse cultures?

This is our world. It is the world of the emerging church. It is in this world that we sit, video remote in one hand and gospel in the other. It is in this world that Jesus walks. And in the explosive mix of sound and text and image, new expressions of church and worship are emerging. Christianity in the West is in decline. Yet in the shadows of the ancient statues of Jesus, new and distinctly Christian approaches to creativity, community, and ritual are being practiced. Christian groups are creatively and imaginatively surfing the postmodern mission edges.

More books

Mike Featherstone, *Consumer Culture and Postmodernism*. London: Sage Publications, 1991.

David Lyon, *Postmodernity*. Buckingham: Open University Press, 1994.

Jean-Francois Lyotard, *The Postmodern Condition. A Report of Knowledge*. Translated by Geoff Bennington and Brian Massumi. Minneapolis, Minn.: University of Minnesota Press, 1984.

Angela McRobbie, *Postmodernism and Popular Culture*. London; New York: Routledge, 1994.

Richard J. Middleton and Brian J. Walsh, *Truth is Stranger Than It Used to Be: Biblical Faith in a Postmodern Age*. Downers Grove, Ill.: InterVarsity, 1995.

Alan Roxburgh, *Reaching a New Generation: Strategies for Tomorrow's Church*. Vancouver, British Columbia: Regent College Publishing, 1993.

Ziauddin Sardar, *Postmodernism and the Other: The New Imperialism of Western Culture*. London/Sterling, Victoria: Pluto Press, 1998

Ziauddin Sardar, *The A to Z of Postmodern Life: Essays on Global Culture in the Noughties*. London: Vision, 2002.

How do I feel after reading Steve's first "postcard"? I feel informed—Steve is a reliable guide who "feels" things as often as he "understands" them, and I tend to think his feelings can be trusted.

I feel relaxed. This new landscape is what it is. We don't need to fear it, nor demonize it, nor panic that we must instantly respond. We can take our time; listen awhile; wait to hear the whispers of the breeze of God blowing across these new fields.

I feel hopeful. Steve is one of many "playing" at the fringes of this new world, trying hard to pick up its tunes and sing them back; believing all the time that the translatability of God has not out-reached itself, that these tribes can also be a womb for the seed of the gospel. I'm looking forward to the journey—and the postcards that will follow.
—Gerard Kelly

Hi from Sydney, Australia. I have just been to visit Café Church in an inner city suburb called Glebe.

They meet in a 100-year-old church building. It's a fantastic space; a high ceiling and plain white walls. Is this the future church, an emerging generation moving into the dying spaces of a church historic?

The night I visited, people were seated café style around tables and in armchairs. There was discussion, candles, projected visuals, and some awesome sax playing. I left with a very real sense of experiencing Christianity true to the life, world, and reality of being 20-something today. How to authentically describe what God is doing in our world today?

1565N

POST CARD

Postcard 2:
Edges of Culture

Early in my PhD study, I came across the writings of a French Jesuit, Michel de Certeau.[28] He explored how the seventeenth century mystics, who lived in times of cultural change and operated on the edges of the church, reconfigured their faith into something vital and life giving. He began to view the edges, both of culture and of the church, as occasions of opportunity rather than crisis. He began to see those who surf the edges as creative and vital renewers of faith. In times of cultural fragmentation, he observed, new and creative life emerged on the edges.

In May 1968, de Certeau got caught up in the student and worker riots in France. The voices of institution and tradition were ignored. The surface appearance of a unified culture was shattered into fragments. He sought to make sense of the decimated storefronts, the riots, and the student protest. He sensed that he was no longer researching historical cultural change, but that he himself was now immersed in a significant cultural shift.

A few years later, in 1974, de Certeau was employed by the French government to research how people responded to contemporary culture. He began to wonder if the emerging world of postmodern culture would engulf ordinary people. How would people respond to a changing cultural context? And where, amid cultural change, should he look to find his answers?

Culture from below

Applying what he learned from his study of the seventeenth century mystics, de Certeau looked at people on the edges. He looked for new life. He looked at how people recombine the fragments of the culture around them.

leaders:
I remember being at a workshop on leadership at which a nun drew a diagram of how different human systems connect. Neat circles intersected in different ways until she drew a line flying off the edge into a different orbit. "That's where real leaders usually find themselves," she commented, "out on the edge, both marginalized and admired by those who manage the systems." I've often wondered how we can live with this reality while still remaining incarnationally located in the center (not as the center of attraction, but being more obviously and easily integrated into other people's lives and ways of being).
—Olive Drane

trackback: Trackback is what we do with the cultural forms that are part of the shift from a consumer society to a culture of co-authorship. Musicians now encourage "remashing" of their own music, and filmmakers create videos with the expectation of future modifications. Writers, who contribute to the grand hypertexted encyclopedia that we call the Internet, write in such a way as to make it easy for others to bookmark, to cross-link, trackback, leave comments, as well as set up systems to maintain communication through the upgrades and additions.
—Andrew Jones

He explored the numerous transformative processes by which individuals creatively subvert the external influence of popular culture.[29]

For de Certeau, the only way to understand properly the impact of cultural change was to look not only at the external inputs, but also at what people did with them. Discussion of cultural change should focus not only on the content of the video or the TV program. It must also consider what people do with what they watch, how they use the remote and the video recorder, how they verbally respond and later reflect over the workroom table.

Culture does not drip down from the top, delivered to the masses down under in some predetermined form. Instead, de Certeau pointed out that culture is never stagnant. As it reaches the crowds, culture is broken apart and remade.

We are, in a way, cultural DJs. Each of us is constantly recording fragments of programs and proverbs, songs and stories. These are mixed into a private multimedia library called the brain. It has been said that there is nothing new under the sun. Creativity does not emerge from nothing. Rather it "is the act of reusing and recombining . . . materials. Meaning is tied to the significance that comes from this new use."[30]

Sure, here in New Zealand Nike and McDonalds have dripped down, wrapping themselves around our billboards and lampposts. But following de Certeau, we need to consider what people do with the external input. We need to look at the way Nike shoes move to a Pacific beat or how local graffiti artists tag McDonalds' logos. Look at the people. Consider what they are doing in response to the external inputs of popular culture.

After trawling for examples from a range of geographical and chronological sources, de Certeau reached a conclusion that has special resonance for those of us exploring what it means to recreate the church in a postmodern era. Dominated but never conquered, groups combine. They keep alive their memories. They creatively take the imposed frames of reference—including those imposed by the church—and reemploy them for their own identity.

It is easy to wring our hands and moan about the polluting effect of contemporary culture. It is tempting to fear for the future of the gospel amid the onslaught of popular culture. But de Certeau gave me faith; cultural shift provides opportunity.

The view from the hairdresser

In order to name this cultural shift, de Certeau applied the labels of "strategy" and "tactics." Strategies are the ways institutions seek to organize a stable reality. Tactics are what people do with these external strategies in everyday life.

My hairdresser provided me with a wonderful example of a grassroots tactical recombination of an institutional strategy. She grew up in a rural New Zealand town. When I told her I was a Baptist pastor, she told me she loved Baptist churches. However, to my surprise, it was not the local youth group that had captured her heart. Instead, it was the second-hand clothing shop.

As she calmly snipped, she told me how this Baptist second-hand clothing shop allowed her to customize her wardrobe. Finding cheap clothes, she would stitch and tuck, creating something new and wanted out of something old and cast aside.

My hairdresser's rural Baptist church chose a strategy of running a second-hand clothing shop as a community ministry. My hairdresser chose a tactic of sampling these clothes and creatively transforming them into something new. While her use of this resource was likely not what the church intended, it remained beneficial to her.

This story is a reminder that when I look at the emerging culture, I need to follow de Certeau's lead and look at people—who are creative, resilient, and capable of surprising acts of re-formation. To put this in distinctly Christian terms, people are made in the

matrix of meaning: Co-authorship was reflected in the way we experienced *The Matrix* films.

Matrix 1, 1999: Within a week of its theatrical release, we e-mailers started a discussion that continued for two months.

Matrix 2, 2002: Within a week of its theatrical release, we bloggers posted entries that added to our interpretation and appreciation of the movie. It lasted a few days.

Matrix 3, 2003: Within a week of its theatrical release, we VJs had access to enough footage to reuse the parts of the movie in our own presentations. Even before its release, we could download the movie trailer files, edit, modify, and reuse them in totally different ways.

Matrixonline.com, 2004: Within a week of the matrixonline.com game release, we gamers will have another playground, another world, another community in which we can play and live. Within six years, we have moved from Consumer, to Commenter, to Co-author, to Citizen.
—Andrew Jones

image of God. This is every individual's default setting. In response to a rapidly changing world, people, made in God's image, creatively "make do," sampling from the world around them. In response to the changes of popular culture, emerging Christians remix what is given to them. They pull existing forms from their external world to create distinctly new ways of following Jesus.

As part of my research for my PhD, I traveled extensively, exploring the lives and worship of the emerging church. After surveying missional innovation around New Zealand, I focused on Cityside Baptist in Auckland, which had a reputation for innovation. This included their version of the Stations of the Cross. Using contemporary icons to reflect on Easter, this artistic project had earned mainstream media coverage and national TV coverage. An inner-city church previously in decline, Cityside was growing, with 50 percent of its attendees between the ages of 20 and 30.[31]

How did this declining church reemerge? The arts were essential. The minister, Mark Pierson, told me, "From the beginning I wanted it to be a place that was open and accepting to artists. I didn't know what that meant really because I've never been an artist, never had any artistic ability . . . I just had this sense that this group of people weren't represented in the church and I'd hear stories from people of how badly they were being treated in the church."[32]

In practice this involved sponsoring an artists' network, called Kissing Hot Coals, to encourage and network Christians involved in the arts. One year the church newsletter featured a series of differently sized blank shapes under the heading, "Cityside supports the arts." People were invited to use the shapes in any way they wanted: they could design a layout for the Cityside building to help seat more people, interpret what was going through the minds of other people, or draw a border to go with a prayer. These efforts to encourage artistic imagination fueled the growth and impact of the church.

The Stations of the Cross became an invitation to congregational members to present a historic Christian Station in a contemporary fashion. People who felt relegated to the edges of most Christian communities were invited to creatively engage with the Christian story and the Christian tradition. When this marginalized group, poorly represented and poorly treated by the church, was given creative space, it blossomed into a faith community that is changing its city.

Israel on the edge

These insights were food for thought. I started to see the emerging church as part of a long history of God-inspired apostolic endeavor. Consider Israel, a community born in the borderlands of slavery. On the margins of the desert, a new code of behavior evolved. The Torah, the first five books of the Bible, emerged as a guide for communal living on the edge. Follow God, Israel, because you as a people were marginal slaves in Egypt. Protect the marginal people, Israel, because you as a people were alien in Egypt.[33] For Israel the borderland of the desert became the seedbed of a new communal future.

Hundreds of years later, Israel again entered the borderlands. In exile, they experienced life on the edge marked by alienation, by exclusion. The nation of Israel cried: How could we sing the Lord's song in a foreign land?[34] In exile, Israel picked over the fragmented and shattered edges of its understanding of God. The strategies of the temple institution were inaccessible. Yet from this experience on the edge, Jewish faith was revitalized. It moved from temple to synagogue. It tactically initiated patterns that sustained it through centuries of life in the midst of other nations and other faiths.

There is also an interesting interplay between the chaos of the edge and the brooding and breathing Spirit. In Genesis 1 the Spirit of God hovers over uncreated chaos and God's good and creative work emerges. The next mention of the Spirit is another borderland experience. As the people of God journey in the wilderness, the Spirit of God

edge: cutting edge, bleeding edge, over the edge, lunatic fringe, back of beyond, whoop whoop, middle of nowhere, end of the earth, event horizon, far perimeter, margins, isolation, the colonies, the western front, the boundary, avant-garde, beyond here, there be monsters . . .

next, fresh, exhilarating, frightening, unknown, suspicious, untried, fashionable, a fad, future, ephemeral, unreachable, unsustainable, incomprehensible, uncomfortable, unacceptable, dangerous, creative, cool, distanced, embraced, ridiculed, approached, imagined, passed.
—Cathy Kirkpatrick

on the bookshelf:
Paul Hanson. *The People Called: The Growth of Community in the Bible.* San Francisco: Harper and Row, 1986.

in the CD player:
Derek Lind, *12 Good Hours of Daylight,* Someone Up There Records, 2002.

language: At Pentecost, each person heard his or her own tongue. What would that mean for postmodern people? What are the sights and sounds and experiences through which postmodern people will hear in their own tongues?
—John and Olive Drane

danger zone: If you walk along the edge, you cannot avoid being cut. As with the old saying (from Matthew 21:43), "Everyone who falls on that stone will be broken to pieces, but he on whom it falls will be crushed." One way or another, change will visit you.

As long as there are centers, there will be edges.

Time moves from now, away, to the event horizon. Once there it faces a new skyline. The surest way of discovering that you are at an edge is by falling off. But considering that the heart of our religion is death, resurrection, and the implicit change, what is there to fear?
—Cathy Kirkpatrick

gives "ability and intelligence, with knowledge and all craftsmanship."[35] As the disciples waited in the shadow of the cross, resurrection, and ascension, the Spirit of God broke through. The book of Acts tells of the evolution of the church as the Spirit falls and the body is transformed.

Border country

I just bought a new piece of art painted by Derek and Nic Lind, a father and son. On one half, in bright reds and yellows, is written "Border Country" and the phrase "I'm a' learn me the language." On the other half, in somber black, is a line from a Bruce Springsteen song: "Mister state trooper, please don't stop me."[36]

I am drawn to the red and yellow side. I have chosen to "learn me the language" of postmodernism. In many ways it feels like "border country." The state troopers told me not to go there, that postmodernity is the badlands. I have been warned of the dangers of being both postmodern and Christian. I might slip into syncretism. I might lose my faith.

Yet I am drawn to the border country. Michel de Certeau would tell me I'm drawn to border country because the edges are seedbeds of the future. He would encourage me: "Every culture proliferates along its margins."[37] The borderlands are the places of greatest creativity.

The Scriptures tell me that God has always been at the edges. As Christianity in the West declines and faith is marginalized, perhaps it isn't so dangerous to seek the Spirit on the borders. As I look at the borders and edges, I see poets, prophets, and apostles finding and showing me God. I see the Spirit of God, brooding and breathing. In the ways of God, the emerging church might yet be the seedbed of a new communal faith.

The postmodern or emerging church runs the risk of being considered a fad or adapted as a surface, sexy, quick-fix technology. It deserves better. The following postcards will articulate the missiology of the emerging church and offer theological resources to nourish, deepen, sustain, and strengthen what God is breathing.

More books

Tom Beaudoin, *Virtual Faith: The Irrevent Spiritual Quest of Generation X*. San Francisco: Jossey-Bass, 1998.

Michel de Certeau, *The Practice of Everyday Life*. Trans. Steven F. Rendall. Berkeley, Calif.: University of California Press, 1984.

John Drane, *The McDonaldization of the Church*. London: Darton, Longman, and Todd, 2000.

Gordon Lynch, *After Religion: "Generation X" and the Search for Meaning*. London: Darton, Longman, and Todd, 2002.

Michael Riddell, Mark Pierson, Cathy Kirkpatrick, *The Prodigal Project*. London: SPCK, 2000.

Alan Roxburgh, *The Missionary Congregation, Leadership, and Liminality*. Valley Forge, Penn.: Trinity Press International, 1997.

Terry Veling and Thomas Groome, *Living in the Margins: Intentional Communities and the Art of Interpretation*. New York: Crossroad Publishing, 1996.

More websites

www.cafechurch.org.au

www.emergingchurch.org

www.emergingchurch.info

www.emergentvillage.com

ritual of new beginnings: Take a packet of fast-growing flowers. Remind the children of the new beginnings they are experiencing. Together, clear the earth in a place you will often pass as a family. Give some seeds to everyone. Plant them together as an act of prayer, that new life will emerge and fresh color will spring forth.

Part Two
Emerging Firestarters

Hi from Edinburgh in Scotland. I've just been enjoying a latte with the Club Culture Project (or Raven). They are a group seeking to live their faith and establish a church among clubbing cultures. The heart of their community is a midday Sunday gathering at a local café. I like the way their life emerges from the cafes, the natural, relational, meeting places of the culture. Again and again in my travels I see God birthing new groups. How could the notion of birth, and midwifing birth, apply to the emerging church?

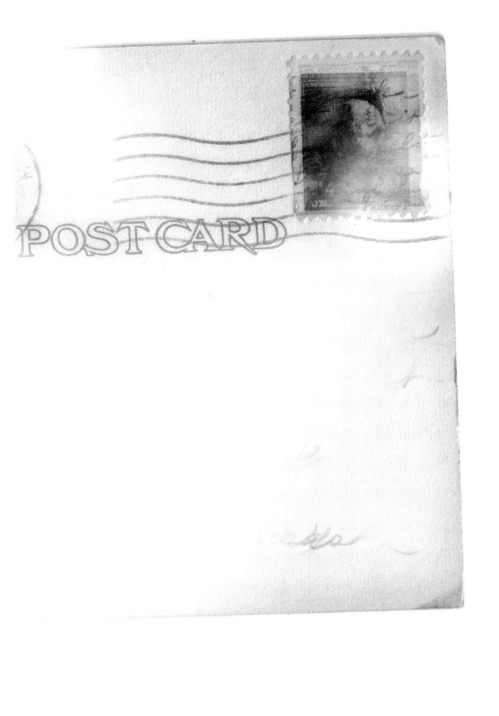

POST CARD

Postcard 3:
Koru Theology

I had a weird moment at my local café today. One of my spiritual disciplines is coffee drinking. It is not just the taste and the space to enjoy life. It is also the chance to be present in my culture. I choose a local café and make it my lounge. It allows me to build relationships where conversations happen. When you're a person of faith, those conversations often get spiritual.

So it was today. The owner of the café asked what I did for a living. I've been in pastoral ministry long enough to know that "I'm a Baptist minister" is usually a conversation killer. But not this time. Hardly pausing for breath, he asked if I believed in "rebirthing." It turned out he was referring to baptism.

I pondered the slip of the tongue. Does God rebirth? What would be the implications of a rebirthing God for the church of the twenty-first century? Such questions are the focus of this postcard.

Learning to create: Koru theology

God is the God of beginnings. At the dawn of the world, God blew the first breath of humanity. As a child is born, the first breath of life is a profoundly spiritual moment. There is something mystical about being part of birth, hearing the first cry, cutting the cord. (I was so moved at the birth of my first daughter

Learning to create: Genesis 2

When the Lord God made the earth
and the heavens
> as the church in the West
> declined and Foucault showed
> the oppressive constructions
> of all our language

and no shrub of the field had yet
appeared on the earth
> for the chasm between rich
> and poor widened and
> refugees begged at Western
> borders

and no plant of the field had yet
sprung up,
> for the soil had become saline
> and pesticides scoured the
> food chain

for the Lord God had not yet sent rain
on the earth
> as acid rain dripped from
> God's creation and humanity
> blistered under a punctured
> ozone layer

and there was no *adam* to work the
ground
> amid a tide of global
> technologies a torrent of
> Internet and wi-fi, images and
> text message

but streams came up from the earth
and watered the ground
> as Derrida deconstructed, DJs
> danced, clubbed their mixes,
> connecting new communities

the Lord God formed the *adam* from
the dust of the ground and breathed
into his nostrils the breath of life and
the *adam* became a living being.

fronds: I like the metaphor of creation and "unfolding fronds" to focus on hope and future possibilities. But I'm also aware of how easy it would be to forget or deny the fact that we have an unavoidable connection to the historical church. Sometimes we'd prefer to cut ourselves free from the institutional church, especially since, at times, its history is nothing to be proud of.

All the same, we aren't born out of nothing. What if we took the metaphor of birth in a slightly different way? What if we think of postmodern culture as the world the "infant" church is being born into, and the womb, the amniotic fluid we are born from, as the historical church? Despite the fact that the traditional church is, in places, sad and old, and despite the fact that some of us have had better "parent" churches than others, we are, nonetheless, the next generation in the history of the church, rather than some brand-new, unprecedented creation.

—Maggi Dawn

that I called her "my wee man." It remains on video for all my family to enjoy.)

In Maori culture, the indigenous culture of New Zealand, new birth is a central motif and is imaged in the *koru*, the unfurling fern. At the heart of a fern sits a tiny curled frond. With space, it unrolls. Over time, it turns from a light and timid green to a dark, rich emerald. And yet the fern cannot grow unless it has a clear path toward the sun. So the Maori burn off undergrowth in order to encourage new life. The cycles of death and decay are the compost of the new. This is koru theology.

New birth is a pervasive biblical image occurring in God's creation, in God's dealings with Israel, and in the life and death of Jesus. The heart of Christian discipleship is God who invites us to be born again. So in John 3:4, the people of God are called to rebirth: "Jesus answered him, 'Very truly, I tell you, no one can see the kingdom of God without being born from above'" (NRSV). In Christian conversion, a new life unfolds as the Creator continues to birth, form, and shape.

A number of Old Testament passages imagine God as a birthing and nursing mother. The songbook of Israel includes a worship song (Psalm 131) in which our relationship with God is like "a weaned child."[38] And in case the image of God as a nursing mother makes you splutter on your coffee, the lyric is repeated— "like a weaned child is my soul within me" (verse 2). Psalm 90:2 describes God as giving birth to the world: "Before the mountains were born or you brought forth the earth and the world, from everlasting to everlasting you are God."

These images of God as birthmother continue in greater detail toward the end of Isaiah. A number of songs, called Servant Songs, are grouped together. The servant is introduced as one in whom God delights (Isaiah 42:1). While some of the lyrics are applied to Jesus, other lyrics describe the "servant" as being like a woman in childbirth: "For a long time I have kept silent, I have been quiet and held myself back. But now, like a woman in childbirth, I cry out, I gasp and pant" (Isaiah 42:14).

In another song, God is described as a breast-feeding mother who would never forget her child (Isaiah 49:15).[39] In Isaiah 44:2, Israel is described as being formed in the womb of God. Then in Isaiah 66:9 the womb of God contracts: "'Do I bring to the moment of birth and not give delivery?' says the Lord, 'Do I close up the womb when I bring to delivery?' says your God."

God gives birth and delights in playing with his children. "You will nurse and be carried on her arm and dandled on her knees. As a mother comforts her child, so will I comfort you."[40]

These biblical texts ask us to rethink our images of God. God is a nurse, a dandler, a comforter, of that which God births.[41]

At the heart of Christian faith, the death and resurrection of Jesus, the life-giving actions of God are described in relation to birth pains: "But God raised him from the dead, freeing him from the agony (*odinas*) of death, because it was impossible for death to keep its hold on him" (Acts 2:24). Elsewhere in the New Testament, the Greek word *odinas* is translated as labor pains; for instance in "destruction will come upon them suddenly, as labor pains (*odinas*) on a pregnant woman" in 1 Thessolonians 5:3; "break forth and cry aloud, you who have no labor pains (*odinas*)" in Galatians 4:27; and the woman who was "pregnant and cried out in pain (*odinas*) as she was about to give birth" in Revelation 12:2.

This birthing imagery is clear in the original Greek, and provides fresh insight into the resurrection. Hence Acts 2:24 can be translated as "God raised him from the dead, freeing him from the labor (*odinas*) of death." New birth is intrinsic to resurrection. God is portrayed as experiencing labor pains and in the resurrection of Jesus we hear the first cry of life. Birth, or koru, theology, is essential to God, who acts in creation, in Israel, and in Jesus' teaching, death, and resurrection.[42]

The feminine: The idea of drawing out the feminine is not a new idea at all; it only seems that way because we've inherited Christianity from the patriarchal world of late modernism and Victoriana. Yet the imagery you are picking up here was commonplace in medieval literature and iconography; Jesus as the breastfeeding Savior was a common image. God as feminine is an idea that has recurred throughout Christian history, just as resistance to it has also recurred. It seems that in the emerging church (and especially in the U.S.) resistance to the feminine is as strong as ever—both as a theological concept and in terms of the acceptance of women as fully participating members of the body of Christ. But I live in hope; there are signs people are engaging with different ways of thinking and being. Maybe the emerging church will be able to grasp a more whole image of God, and deliver some justice for its women.
—Maggi Dawn

to dandle: verb. To move a child lightly up and down in the arms or on the knee. To make much of. *Shorter Oxford English Dictionary.*

Easter Sunday:
a celebration of life
The party lives on

On Friday
angels, stunned in
disbelief
planets, slumped in
meaningless orbit
earth, issuing its
mournful waita*

Til Sunday
when God hauled the
Son to his feet
The giver of life
received the caress
of life
and walked past decay

Every pain
found new meaning
every death found a
new tomorrow
every sin, freshly
cleaned and gutted,
found victory
every evil wink was
exposed
every ruptured,
torn, and tattered
relationship
was renewed

Earth and angel united
in laughing, dancing,
spinning delight

Jesus lives and so life
wins
Did you hear me?
Life wins.

*waita is a Maori word
for song

in the CD player:
"Stuck in A Moment,"
U2, All that You
Can't Leave Behind.
Universal International
Music, UK, 2000.

Learning to birth death to life

If God is about birthing—and rebirthing—and we are to be about the things of God, then we, too, are called to acts that bring new life into the world. For those who are living on and looking at the edges, there are labor pangs all around, cries that need to be heeded if we are to follow God's leading toward new life. It is here—in the delivery room on the borderlands—that the emerging church is finding its mission.

Every birth is marked by a kind of death. A newborn child leaves behind a womb of safety and comfort. In utero, all of the child's needs are met without any effort on the child's part. Yet to come fully into existence, the child must leave this place of safety and move violently into a new kind of life where survival is rather uncertain. There is no birth without loss.

For many in the emerging church, that birthing process is just beginning. Slowly shedding the protective coating that sheltered them for so long, they are baring themselves to the elements. The death of what they once knew can be both devastating and freeing. Yet there is a temptation to move into the new simply because it is not the old.

Terry Veling notes that emerging communities "expend much frustrated energy in trying to escape rather than engage that to which they belong. They see their suspicions, their critiques, their doubts leading them further and further away from tradition, rather than recognizing that their critical reading is part of the ongoing process of interpretation."[43] The irony is that this deconstructive energy cuts off our life-giving potential. The curse of post-evangelicalism is that it knows what it has come from, but seems less certain about what it will become. In the words of Bono, it is easy to get "stuck in a moment."

The move from deconstruction and death to reconstruction and new life is essential. Koru theology invites us to discover "possibilities of who we might become, rather than dwelling on who we have been."[44] It invites us to newness, to rebirth, to re-creation even in the face of death. The brokenness of the past can lead to wholeness in the future.

The birthing of communities

One of the mystical and spiritual strands of the birth experience is the fragility and uniqueness of each new life. Birth is about the separation of one life from another, the emergence of a distinct, finite individual. We can only hold the newly born because of an act of separation and dislocation. As the child grows, it increasingly separates from its parents. Fast-forward to the teenage years when the dislocation from parents is essential to social and spiritual development of a unique personality. In order to be authentically life giving, koru theology must also embrace this sense of the unique.

Similarly, emergent communities in the midst of the birthing process need to come to life with a sense of fragility and individuality. Modernity asked us to hand over our individuality for the sake of being fused into a common community. Overarching labels, or metanarratives, were created. Communities were birthed that, unlike human birth or God birth, did not honor individuality. Rather they started with communion and commonality. This was the era of the rise of nation states, in which a common bond was sought for the good of the whole. The recent tragedies in Rwanda and the Balkans show the finite nature of these modern visions of community.

French thinker Jean-Luc Nancy focuses on this rupture of community. He argues that the experience of being human is not that of being in common, but that of being separate.

A healthy part of human development is for babies and teenagers to become distinct from their parents. Maturity is becoming aware of our differences and facing our own mortality. As we come to terms with our uniqueness and distance from others, so we are able to see the uniqueness and distance in others. This allows

on the bedside table: Jean-Luc Nancy. *The Inoperative Community*, ed Peter Connor, trans, Peter Connor, et al. Minneapolis: University of Minnesota Press, 1991.

dislocation: So spacious is he, so roomy, that everything of God finds its proper place in him without crowding. Not only that, but all the broken and dislocated pieces of the universe—people and things, animals and atoms—get properly fixed and fit together in vibrant harmonies, all because of his death, his blood that poured down from the Cross.
—from Colossians 1, *The Message*

sea glass mosaic: When I was in Gisborne over the summer I collected lots of sea glass off the beach. I reflected on Colossians 1 where it says that God will take all the broken and dislocated pieces of the universe and fit them together in vibrant harmonies. Perhaps God will fit them together in some new mosaic rather than simply using superglue to stick it all back together as it was.
—Lynne Taylor, emergentkiwi.org.nz

flame:
flame
flickers by open door
swirls in Desert Draught
gulps, greedy, for Breath

flame
atop wrought black candlestand
amid flatpack saucer
afloat in scented water
lights of Breath, resting amid differently shaped wax
beaded, twisted, sprawled
cross crusted table
smelling of coffee, dregs and dust
up long, up late, listening to table,
talk of reality

O God, Flame of love
Set the creatives alight
Fan into flame differently shaped churches
for our multibox world
Amen.

what Nancy calls a "being in common," a community formed from shared uniqueness and attention to dislocation, both ours and others'.[45]

I wonder if this is what happened at the Last Supper. Jesus is with friends. It is the last meal. Imagine if Jesus stood up with a motivational speech to emphasize the common pool of shared vision. Instead, Jesus is attentive to brokenness. He speaks of "betrayal" and "suffering," words heavy with loss. He takes, and breaks, bread. This is a community attentive to dislocation.

Yet out of this shared brokenness, the church as community is born. Because Jesus acknowledges the brokenness of life, he then births a community that shares deeply without demanding the loss of one's identity. It is a community that will grow and develop, aware of its own humanity, which in turn allows it to be attentive to the brokenness of others. A missional heart can beat in this experience of community.

The need for midwives

Before the birth of our first child, the midwife warned me about something called transition in labor. In transition, the cervix is almost fully dilated and the woman giving birth has the overwhelming desire to push but premature pushing can cause damage. Some fairly frank things can be said during this part of the birth process.

Culturally we are in a time of transition. Some of us love Zeffarelli's version of *Romeo and Juliet*. Parts of Western culture are aging, and mission to Zeffarelli's world remains an important dimension. Equally, others of us are born into Luhrmann's world.

The church is experiencing this transition as well. When to push toward birth and when not to push? Some things said in transition are best left in the birthing unit. Times of transition require grace, sensitivity, and multiple mission strategies. They require the help of midwives.

In 1999, I surveyed more than 100 young church leaders in New Zealand and asked them what they needed from established churches and leaders. Seventy-five percent of them asked for help. They wanted a midwife. What was even more staggering was that 96 percent defined their request for support in relational terms: people to give encouragement, recognition, and credibility. They didn't want books or formulas or models, they wanted mentors, friends, companions.

One young leader expressed it vividly. She demanded that Gen X-ers be apprenticed. "The baby boomer way of running organizations scares me . . . all these big boys of mission . . . [they need to] involve us, apprentice us."[46] The emerging church is asking for help in the form of relational partnering in birthing what God is conceiving in them.

The midwife image brings a number of birth issues into focus. The primary task of a midwife is to ensure the healthy birth of the baby. This is paramount. But there is also a willingness to be part of the mess and anxiety and an ability to work with a range of people—a pregnant mother in various stages of emotion, a helpless-feeling father (speaking from personal experience), various family members, and, if necessary, a range of other medical professionals.

Among emerging churches there are some skilled midwifes who are demonstrating this same willingness. They have taken midwifery seriously and are providing life-giving services.[47] The Baptist Union of Victoria in

Natural timing:
Labor and birth are
unique to each person.
No two are the same.
Each needs to be
traveled through
and approached
differently. The
midwife needs
patience to allow the
labor to unfold and
progress. Allowing
labor to unfold
naturally without
pressure allows the
woman to release
endorphins (natural
pain relief) into the
bloodstream. Trying
to rush, pressure, or
force the mother into
a situation she is not
comfortable with may
slow, or even stop,
labor.
—Kathryn Fromont,
midwife

Australia is one such example.[48] They have courageously committed themselves to identifying, nurturing, and providing resources for 20 experimental church plants over the next five years. The key word is *experimental*. There is an understanding that some of these "births" will be complicated, that some will thrive while others need intensive care.

The Baptist Union has chosen to foster innovation by commissioning a "New Missional Communities" group that provides funding and carefully studies each innovation. This funding is based on loose and flexible criteria to encourage innovation. It is the equivalent of one year's full-time salary, but is allocated according to the mission of the group. It has gone toward property, toward accommodations, and toward salaries.

In addition, the Union offers administrative help and has set up support forums to bounce around ideas. These forums are a place for key denominational leaders to provide pastoral support and champion innovation, increasing the sense of connection between experimental emerging groups and the denomination.

One of the beneficiaries of this intentional midwifery process is the LivingRoom, which meets in inner city Melbourne for a weekly vegetarian meal. Founder Darren Rowse says that because of the denominational midwifery of the Baptist Union he feels as though the LivingRoom is "a legitimate and important part of the denomination" and part of a wider church family "inspired to dream of new ways of connecting with our culture."[49]

Another example of such midwifery is occurring in the Anglican Dioecese of Oxford in England. In 2003, all the dioceses in England received some unexpected funds.[50] The Diocese of Oxford had already been exploring new mission possibilities and the implications for the Parish system in a more tribal generation. The Diocese of Oxford chose to use the money to form Cutting Edge Ministries, with the intention of developing new expressions of church.

In this case, midwifery involved funding a number of new forms of church. Financial support was provided on a sliding scale, with the goal of the recipients becoming self-sufficient within four years. The diocese also set up meetings to network these new forms of church with one another. They commissioned "accompaniers," people with expertise in certain areas who could provide support and help. One of the results is mayBe, a new alternative church group in Oxford committed to community, creativity, and simplicity, working toward a café-music-art-prayer-worship space in a street front location.

Stretch marks

Midwifery has been a stretching experience. But the more births take place, the more these midwifing denominations are learning. The flexibility of their funding is constantly challenged, as imaginative proposals push traditional shapes of church. They are learning that birthing means risk and that not all risks work.

They are also learning the gestation period can't be hurried. Anne Wilkinson Hayes from the Baptist Union of Victoria says, "Sometimes it feels as if it is ages—certainly more than nine months—between the time an idea is first brought to our group and actually seeing the head! My temptation is to get people to push too soon, but this involves a lot of wasted effort and sometimes even damage. There is no hurry and it takes time for things to emerge organically rather than programmatically."

Midwives must respect the uniqueness of the baby and the birthing experience. They put a range of support structures in

a church called mayBe:
community, creativity, simplicity

- mayBe is a community to be part of, rather than a church to go to.
- mayBe is very "fuzzy" at the edges, while drawing on monastic and contemporary community roots so people can commit themselves to this particular rhythm of life and community.
- The heart of our life will be in small groups gathering around shared food and drink.
- Each group will seek its place of presence and mission calling in the wider community.
- The whole community will gather frequently for worship in "the big expression."
- mayBe is not just a Sunday experience. The community will develop a prayerful rhythm of life throughout the week.
- mayBe will feel very contemporary, yet will draw on ancient Christian symbols and patterns of life.
- Creativity is high profile and open to all, producing imaginative resources for the spiritual journey.
- This will be a community where the paradoxes are held and honored—exuberant worship and listening prayer, strong faith and tough questions, praise and lament.

A long-term dream: a café-music-art-prayer-worship place in a street front location. Learn more about this church at www.maybe.org.uk.

place before, during, and after the birth. Ann Wilkinson notes, "Birth is a difficult and messy process and traditionally labor has been a more communal event than the privatized affair women experience in Western society. We needed to be more present for those groups who feel the loneliness of birthing something new. We needed to create a more encouraging and safer space for people to vent their frustrations, test their ideas, and share their amazement. This has been very time-consuming in some cases but also very life-giving."

The belief in God's constant re-creation drives much of the emerging church. It is less a reaction against old forms and ideas and more a response to God's call for us to join in with the continuous birthing of his kingdom. It is a turning toward the edge, toward the borderlands, rather than a simple turning against the center. To take part in the rebirthings of God is the privilege of all who are called to be God's people.

mothers: The unwieldy, old-fashioned church communities we've emerged from are like mothers—some supportive and helpful; others worn out, not well, depressed; all of them carrying a certain amount of history and baggage with them (because that's the price of growing up). Of course we should grow up and do our generation's thing. That's what parents want deep down. But let's remember to be kind to the mother church—without her we wouldn't be here.
—Maggi Dawn

More books

John Drane and Olive Fleming Drane, *Family Fortunes: Faith-full Caring for Today's Families.* London: Darton, Longman, and Todd, 2004.

Olive Drane, *Clowns, Storytellers, Disciples: Spirituality and Creativity for Today's Church.* Minneapolis, Minn.: Augsburg, 2004.

Margaret L. Hammer, *Giving Birth: Reclaiming Biblical Metaphor for Pastoral Practice.* Louisville, Ky.: Westminster/John Knox Press, 1994.

Jean-Luc Nancy. *The Inoperative Community*, ed. Peter Connor, trans, Peter Conner, et al. Minneapolis, Minn.: University of Minnesota Press, 1991.

More websites

www.gospeltruth.net/allen/spon_expanofch.htm

www.picnmix.com/blogger.html

Hi from York (UK). I trained down from Edinburgh and have just been at Visions. They meet in St. Cuthberts, an Anglican church, parts of which date back to 687 AD. It's a great space with a tremendous sense of ancient spirituality.

The striking thing about Visions is their use of visuals. First it was multiple projectors. Now it is video loops. In a world gone visual, Visions' visuals are a superb example of creative Christian faith. What is the place of creativity in the emerging church? What is the impact of a visual faith in our visual world?

2833

Post Card

U.S. POSTAGE

THIS SPACE FOR ADDRESS ONLY

1—

Postcard 4:
Creativity Downloaded

In many ways, the emerging church is a community at play. Rather than sticking with an existing or inherited theology, the emerging church understands theology as a place for innovation and the fresh breathings of God. That doesn't mean there is a discounting of history and previous good theology. It means there is a recognition that, time and again, the chaos of cultural change is a God-given space for creative innovation. There is room in the theology of the emerging church for the creative power of God.

A theology of creativity starts with the Spirit of God.[51] In Genesis 1:2 "the Spirit of God was hovering over the waters," an active presence that suggests creativity is in the very essence of God. In Exodus 35:30-32, Bezalel, son of Uri, is filled with "the Spirit of God, with skill, ability and knowledge in all kinds of crafts—to make artistic designs for work in gold, silver and bronze" for use in the tabernacle. Others in the community are Spirit-skilled as weavers, designers, and craftsmen to construct the sanctuary. Here, creative work in the church on behalf of the community of God is powered by the Spirit.

A theology of creativity continues with the Son: "In the beginning was the Word" (John 1:1). Clement of Alexandria, an ancient theologian offers an inspiring interpretation of the creativity of Christ:

> The Word sings according to a new harmony, a musical mode which bears the name of God; he has submitted the dissonance of the elements to the discipline

move ahead: The modern church possesses an almost prohibition-like spirit against innovation. Within its pragmatic, utilitarian confines, generative activity is often looked upon as frivolous. Superfluous. As if God's creative work ceased on the seventh day, and our task as humans is but to harness the finished, divine product to meet our basic needs. The philosophy in summary: If creation is finished, then human innovation is a waste of time. Yet, it does not take much Scripture to dispel the heresy of a finished creation. Whether it is Miriam free-composing a ballad at the crossing of the Red Sea, or the Apostle Paul recontextualizing Athenian poetry for the sake of unbelievers, the seventh day was only the beginning. Innovation is the way we stamp God's image onto the work of our hands.
—Sally Morgenthaler

in the CD player: Moby, "God Moving over the Face of the Waters," *I Like to Score—Music from Films Vol. 1*, Elektra Entertainment Group, 1997.

of musical harmony to make a symphony of the whole world. Like the Word, Christ is son, music. No true music ever existed before him. As for us, we were already music before any other music; for we were in Christ before time began.[52]

Yet the Word is not the only biblical way to describe Jesus. In Colossians 1:15, Christ is the *eikon*, the image of God. We have spent many a theological year dining out on God as Word only. Mitchell Stephens points out that we are inhabitants of a Western culture that historically has had an "almost unbiblical allegiance to the word," accompanied by an "antagonism toward images."[53] In digesting only the idea of the Word and all its concreteness, we have lost much of the beauty of the image, the imaginative, the visceral. We need to compensate by spending many a year tasting of God as Image.

God, whether Father or Creator, Son or Redeemer, Spirit or Sustainer, is creative. As bearers of the image of God (Genesis 1:26), we too are to live out the creativity of God. An essential missionary tool for the emerging church is to follow a God of creativity in a personal rediscovery of what it means to be a people of godly play.

Recent theological mountains have been shaped by rational thought and based upon many a lengthy word. They have thrown the chill of a long and rational shadow over us. A theology of creativity will require further excavation. So consider with me some images of God.[54] Dr. Robert Banks discusses the many ways in which God acts with creative energy. In his book, *God the Worker*, Banks discusses God as a musician and composer, designer and garment maker, architect and builder, crafter and artisan.

God as musician and composer

Anyone who listens to God's creation—the dawn chorus, the chirp of cicada and cricket, the cry of gull, the roar of sea—will hear God as musician and composer. God rejoices with singing in Zephaniah 3:17, gives a song of comfort in Psalm 42:8, and composes a song of witness in Deuteronomy 31:19.

In Job 38:7, God reminds Job that "the morning stars sang together" at the dawn of Creation. This is most eloquently captured in C. S. Lewis's book, *The Magician's Nephew*, where Digby watches creation being sung to life:

> In the darkness something was happening at last. A voice had begun to sing . . . There were no words. There was hardly a tune. But it was, beyond comparison, the most beautiful noise he had ever heard. It was so beautiful.[55]

The call of Creator and the response of Creation harmonize over the next 15 pages of C. S. Lewis's book. This call and response is a haunting textual melody in which God the Creative Composer sings creation into existence.

The Creator God's ending will be a musical composition as well. When the people of God are free, living fully as God intended, then creation will harmonize and trees will clap the beat (Isaiah 55:12). Music is woven into the book of Revelation, including choir (5:9ff), trumpet (8:6), thunder clap (10:3), and harp (14:2).

One of my favorite spiritual spots is a monastery in the middle of the city of Auckland. It includes old, old trees and lush green grass that runs downhill to meet acres of house and street. I hug those trees and sit on those hills. I hear God sing in the psalm, "The meadows are covered with flocks and the valleys are mantled with grain; they shout for joy and sing" (Psalm 65:13). I align myself with the musical energy of God.

God as designer and dresser

An early glimpse of God shows him clothing humanity by making clothes out of animal skins in Genesis 3:21.

applause: When you [God's people] are set free, you will celebrate and travel home in peace. Mountains and hills will sing as you pass by, and trees will clap.
—Isaiah 55:12, CEV

godly play: When you come to preach Genesis 1, throw away your exegesis and your notes. Give everyone a small square tile and pottery paint. Turn on Moby's "God Moving over the Face of the Waters." Invite people to "create" as you read to them. Mount the tiles as your creation psalm.

revelation and rhythm: Find a musical friend. Select a few texts from Revelation. Then try to express an exegesis of them, not in words, but in music. Find the textual rhythm. Build in the emotion.

God acts as both designer and dresser, mixing creativity with the practical task of equipping people to face their changed world. What a nurturing image of God.

In Psalm 139:15, we read of God weaving us together in the womb. A similar creative image appears in Job 10:11 as Job calls out to God with the humility of knowing that it was God who "knit [him] together with bones and sinews."

Elsewhere in the Old Testament, God lovingly bathes and dresses the orphaned child Jerusalem, then prepares her like a bride:

> I bathed you with water and washed the blood from you and put ointments on you. I clothed you with an embroidered dress and put leather sandals on you. I dressed you in fine linen and covered you with costly garments. I adorned you with jewelry: I put bracelets on your arms and a necklace around your neck, and I put a ring on your nose, earrings on your ears and a beautiful crown on your head. So you were adorned with gold and silver; your clothes were of fine linen and costly fabric and embroidered cloth. Your food was fine flour, honey and olive oil. You became very beautiful and rose to be a queen. (Ezekiel 16:9-13)

Similar themes appear in Isaiah 61:10, where God's salvation and righteousness are the very clothes Israel wears. There is a special resonance to the image of God as the one who clothes us. Banks expresses the connection like this:

> Clothes directly cover our skin. They are the most intimate extensions of ourselves. It is not surprising that they should become the focus of so many hopes and desires. This explains why clothing so easily becomes a metaphor for a whole range of processes, but none so significant as its Old Testament usage—becoming a new person.[56]

This is the creative work of God as designer and dresser. But God's work here is not simply functional. Instead, God plays in a process charged with beauty, richness, and the luxurious imagination of the Creator.

God as architect and builder

God lays the earth's foundations in Psalm 102:25 and builds the earth like a home in Psalm 104:5. In 1 Chronicles 28 we read of God's plans for crafting sacred buildings and furniture for the temple.

In the New Testament, the church is God's building (Matthew 16:18; 1 Corinthians 3:10-17). A more human image of the church comes through in 1 Corinthians 12, with God as the designer and crafter of the complex body that is the church.

The image of God as builder culminates in the picture of the City of God found in Revelation 21–22. The heavenly city is architecturally stunning. It is crafted from rich stones and brilliant jewels and lit up by God's own glorious presence. No architect, no planner, no builder ever conceived a construction on this scale or of this quality.[57]

God as crafter and artisan

One of Christchurch's most popular tourist attractions is Christchurch's Arts Centre. Whenever I wander through it, I see craftwork of all kinds. I look at the weaving and bone carving, the wood turning and painting, the use of bead and metal to form contemporary jewelry. As I smell the leather and appreciate the colors, I consider the crafting, the hands that carefully molded wet clay into a sturdy pitcher, the eyes that chose the orange thread to suggest fire and home. The art tells me about the artist.

God is often described as one who crafts beautiful objects—animals, planets, human beings, his own Word. In Psalm 12:6 God's Word is compared to pure silver, refined over time and with great effort: "The words of the Lord are flawless, like silver refined in a

heaven or earth: My favorite story of the power of beauty to form faith is taken from a Russian story. *The Primary Chronicle* tells of Vladimir, prince of Kiev, who sent several of his followers in search of true religion. First, they went to the Moslem Bulgars of the Volga, but found "no joy," only a "mournfulness and a great smell." Then they went to Germany and Rome and found the worship more satisfactory, but still lacking in beauty. Finally they came to Constantinople, and attending the Church of the Holy Wisdom, they discovered what they were seeking. Consequently, they reported to Vladimir. "We knew not whether we were in heaven or on earth, for surely there is no such splendour or beauty anywhere upon earth. We cannot describe it to you; only this we know; that God dwells there among men, and that their service surpasses the worship of all other places. For we cannot forget that beauty" (cited in Timothy Ware, *The Orthodox Church.* Baltimore: Penguin Books, 1963, p. 269).
—Robert Webber

come: Come to the Lord and Giver of Life. Come to the Spirit, who transforms you from a "lump of clay" to a living being, a person. Come to the Spirit to be refreshed, renewed, restored. —David Adam. *The Cry of the Deer: Meditations on the Hymn of St Patrick.* SPCK: London, 1987, p. 15.

surfing in cyberspace: Go play at www.neave.com

furnace of clay, purified seven times." In Isaiah 48:10, God's work in the hearts of God's people is seen as a process of purification: "I have refined you...in the furnace of affliction." [58]

A similar creative image, God as potter, is one of the classic metaphors for God's relationship to humanity. The earth is fashioned by God's hands (Isaiah 45:18).[59] Adam is formed from the dust of the earth (Genesis 2:7). Isaiah, Jeremiah, and the Apostle Paul all talk of God as the potter and humanity as the clay, molded and shaped by the hands of a master crafter.[60]

God at play

There are elements of play intrinsic to these ideas of God as a creative artist. There is a sense of God's delight in the very process of creating. God has gone beyond a functional creation, choosing instead to design and decorate in order that creation might bear the image of its majestic Creator.

There is a sad irony in the perception that Christianity is dull, that our sermons and worship are boring or unoriginal. This perception stands in sharp contrast to the vibrancy of the Creator God we worship. I am challenged by the images above, reminded of how creative God is and I'm inspired to echo the creative power of God in the ways I express and share my faith. And I'm not the only one.

Ian Mobsby is planting his second emerging church, Moot, in central London. Moot began in 2003, exploring ways of supporting one another and exploring how to do worship, mission, and community in London's busy and liquid-modern society.[61] Mobsby introduced me to the concept of "godly play," an interactive approach to learning that invites people to creatively, playfully engage with the biblical story. Godly play involves three parts:

The telling, in which a Bible story is told, slowly and respectfully. Often symbols are used to help bring the story to life. I have a large plastic box filled with sand. If I am telling the story of crossing the Jordan, I add rocks for the altar, grapes for the land of milk and honey, a rich blue cloth to represent the river. To prepare for the telling, I read a child's Bible story and then fill it in with scriptural detail. The telling then opens people up to the power of the biblical story.

The questing is an invitation to participate in and wonder about the story. I pause the story and invite those gathered to wonder by asking questions that start with the phrase, "I wonder." I wonder why this happened? I wonder what would happen if this part was not in the story? I wonder how the character felt at this point? I wonder where God was? I wonder where I would be in the story? I wonder where my faith community would be in the story? The questions of wonder are endless and emerge from engagement with the story. The wondering allows people to play with the story and in so doing, to locate themselves within the biblical story.

The ending returns to conclude the story. It allows the text to have priority and can often lead into worship. It also invites multisensory responses, in which space and time is provided for individuals to continue to interact with God in relation to the biblical text.

Godly play originates with Jerome Berryman, who recommends it for children.[62] Yet I watched Ian Mobsby hold 30 young adults and 15 children transfixed for half an hour using the ideas of godly play. No mean feat. I have since used godly play at intergenerational house church gatherings, in classrooms with children, with groups of adult students, and, using live video feeds, to large Sunday congregations. All ages have commented to me on its effectiveness and have appreciated the chance to creatively play within the biblical text.

The poet Angelus Silesius writes, "God plays with creation. All that is play that the deity gives itself. It has imagined the creature for its pleasure."[63]

God plays, not manipulatively, but imaginatively and joyfully. And if we as humans are made in the image of God, then we too are called to play. We are called to delight in the gifts of God, in humanity, in the earth, in the pull of our creative selves.

the squeeze: If God creates in so much diversity, what does God think of the shrinking of both linguistic and environmental diversity? See "For Want of a Word" in *New Scientist* at www.newscientist.com

The Eastern Orthodox Church has a tradition of starting their Easter Sunday services with a round of joke telling.[64] At Graceway we drew from this tradition. We hid Easter eggs, snuggling them into layers and layers of white cloth laid around the edges of the church building. Each Easter egg was wrapped with a joke. We invited people to find the Easter eggs and keep the jokes. Then we gathered and used the jokes as a call to worship; a round of joke telling. The children playfully searched, the community laughed. God plays. The gift of Easter life is the joy-filled call for us to play as well.

In 2001, I interviewed alternative worship leaders in New Zealand, Australia, and the United Kingdom.[65] In each of these conversations, there was a sense that intuitive play was an essential part of life in these communities. One practitioner from the UK told me, "I think people often did not know what the service was going to feel like until it happened. But people were willing to play around and to say, 'Well, who knows what will happen if we run this video clip or commercial next to this sixteenth century religious painting and if we play . . . some weird band underneath it And what will it feel like? Well, let's try and see.'"

The mission of the emerging church starts in cooperation with the God of play. It calls for a willingness to live out the creative *imago Dei* in ways that touch the culture in which we live. I'm not suggesting play as a wanton, unconstrained act of irresponsibility or irreverence. In one sense we as Christians play with a set number of paintbrushes: Scripture, tradition, orthodoxy (the sixteenth century painting). To these we add the unique experiences of life in our world (the video clip, the weird band). Like the Renaissance painters or the early Greek fresco artists, we create out of the belief that God is present in the act of rebirth, of new life.

The front cover of the February 2002 *NZ Marketing Magazine* caught my eye.[66] It was a totally white cover with the words, "Post-modernist marketing. Draw your own cover." Attached was a set of 12 crayons.

Our postmodern culture is asking us to imagine

show me: There is a term in the ancient church that catches the power of the idea that experience precedes thought. It is *lex orandi; lex redendi; est*—the rule of prayer is the rule of faith. Another way of stating this truth is "show me how you worship or live and I will tell you what you believe." In the modern world this axiom was turned around. It was always "get your theology straight and then your praxis will flow from it." In the postmodern world we are rediscovering that experience precedes reflection.

—Robert Webber

new ways of being human. It is asking us to play, to let our imaginations take hold. At the same time, we are the creations of an imaginative, innovative God who begs us to follow in the steps of our Creator. The push to reimagine, to renew, to re-create is all around us. On our right hand, the postmodern culture is inviting us to play. On our left, the gospel of God asks us to play. We are being called by both culture and Christian faith to download creativity.

Yes but . . .

I've been talking about this idea of play long enough to know that it raises concerns for many Christians. There is a fear that "playing" with God and God's Word might take away from the holiness and awesome power of God. Yet I find that creative play in fact allows a fresh, deeper, and more meaningful engagement with Scripture.

One Easter I gave people sand and pipe cleaners and invited them to make the Easter Garden. The first thing people did was ask questions and reach for their Bibles. How many angels were there? How many women were there? A simple invitation to play encouraged much interaction with the Bible.

I also find that there are those who are wary of the arts making their way into worship. For them, this could be the beginning of a slow slide into the creation of graven images and the worship of the human endeavor rather than the Divine.

This question has been a theological arm wrestle throughout history. While Exodus 20:4 instructs us not to make idols, we have the history of the early church, which made artistic images of God.[67] We also have the wisdom of the Eastern Orthodox Church, which has always seen icons as revelatory:

> When he who is bodiless and without form, immeasurable in the boundlessness of His own nature, existing in the form of God, empties Himself and takes the human form of a servant in substance and in stature and is found in a

storytime: I ran a storytelling workshop evening. I matched people in pairs to tell stories of God at work in their lives. Then I asked them to have a go at retelling a Bible story before pulling back to discuss. The key question:

Q. Is it harder to retell Bible stories?
A. Yes. When I tell my own stories, I experienced all the detail. Not so with Bible stories.

Q. So how do we find the detail in Bible stories?
A. Bible atlases and commentaries. The retelling of Bible stories invites us deeper into the Bible world.

for more: See Trevor Hart, "Through the Arts: Hearing, Seeing and Touching the Truth" in *Beholding the Glory: Incarnation Through the Arts,* edited by Jeremy Begbie. Grand Rapids: Baker Books, 2000.

on the bookshelf: Peter Graystone, *Signs of the Times: The Secret Lives of Twelve Everyday Icons,* Norwich: Canterbury Press, 2004.

© Sieger Köder, Abendmahl

body of flesh, then you may draw His image and show it to anyone willing to gaze upon it.[68]

The Christian theology of creation and incarnation affirm the goodness of matter, and thus by implication human creativity and human appreciation of such creativity.

Still others worry that art is too vague, too open to individual interpretation to be a meaningful element of communal worship. But the truth is that people are always interpreting, whether it be icons or images, sermons or stories. When the preacher gets thanked for saying something she never said, an act of interpretation has occurred.

Rather than pretend we don't interpret, we can create space for people to check their interpretation in the body of Christ. For where two or three are gathered, there is the interpretive presence of Jesus. The task facing us is to create church as a space in which, by the use of images, people can allow communal interpretation to occur. Options for this include discussions, forums, Q&A, and online resources. A community of interpretation can enhance and correct individual interpretation.

Of course if we all interpret, we are at risk of constructing God in our image. And yet this danger is not overcome by ceasing construction but by exposing our constructions to other attempts.

One way to do this is to let images question us. Take for example the work of contemporary German artist Sieger Koder. His *The Last Supper* features the disciples around the table and the bread broken. Two hands hold the communion cup above the disciples, and in the communion wine is the reflection of a human face. The reflected face cannot be that of any of the disciples around the table. It is unlikely to be that of Jesus, given the angles. That leaves the face of the viewer.

Thus Koder's art reminds us that images question us. What are we bringing to the table with Jesus? If we are not reflected in the cup, where in the art image would we like to be?

Hence any attempt to image God contextually is in fact an act of God reading us. As we embody God, as we proclaim God in community, God looks back, questioning the church: Is the church fully representing the image of God? Is the church a participatory place where people find their full humanity in Christ? Is the body of God a true *ikon* of God?

Thus the question is not "Will we construct God in our own image?" It is "Will we let the image of God construct us?" It is not the images that are the issue, but the faithfulness of our image making.

Image that: Creativity around us

Contemporary culture has been described as a "Civilization of the Image," one in which we are colonized by the image industry.[69] The overthrow of Saddam Hussein is encapsulated in the image of a toppling statue and a bearded man being examined by doctors. We are fed information and opinion in these images. For some, the priority of image and its ability to form opinion can be viewed as crisis.

Equally, it can be viewed as

art and emotion: David Freedberg argues that images challenge our rationality and invite emotion as part of cognition. *The Power of Images: Studies in the History and Theory of Response,* Chicago; London: University of Chicago Press, 1993, 430.

Roland Barthes suggests that the emotion produced by photographs "reaches down into the religious substance out of which I am moulded . . . Photography has something to do with resurrection." *Camera Lucida: Reflections on Photography.* trans. Richard Howard, New York: Vintage, 1981, 82.

Julia Thomas writes of viewing art: "Spectatorship, then, is more about how the subject is positioned by the visual than about how it has any agency to position itself" (from *Reading Images,* Hampshire; New York: Palgrave, 2001, 2).

the neighborhood: Two photographers spend an afternoon taking photos in the same two-block, urban area. Both use black-and-white film. There is a section of urban renewal happening on one end. The paint on the 1890s houses has been stripped. On several porches, there is fresh paint. Hanging plants adorn the porches of two nearly finished units. A young father is fixing the steps with his three-year-old son in tow. One photographer focuses on this heartwarming scene, capturing a triptych of hope, of a city reborn. The other is fixated on a child playing next to a garbage heap in an alleyway. She has no shoes. Which view, which set of photos, is more faithful? Which realities take precedence? Or can they both be faithful? Who decides?
—Sally Morgenthaler

on the book shelf:
Mitchell Stephens, *The Rise of the Image, the Fall of the Word.* New York: Oxford University Press, 1998.

out the window:
The primary task of evangelism in a postmodern world is to provide a window frame for the shards and fragments of postmodern life. The world needs windows to God. But not as we have done in past eras—unquestioned faith statements, peering down upon the masses who would know nothing unless we enlightened them. No, the world needs to make its own windows. All they need is the trusty framework of God's story, the girders of creation, disorientation, reorientation, and a universe fulfilled. Then, by all that's holy, we need to step back and get out of the way. Let them bring their bits of stories, their questions, doubts, fears, and mostly, that sense of the Other they've already experienced in myriad ways.
—Sally Morgenthaler

possibility, an opportunity to listen to previously unheard questions and unspoken answers. Images lie side by side, disconnected. What connections will we make?

Images are searching for a narrative that will hold and explain them. Hence cultural philosopher Richard Kearney describes the imagination as forever in crisis and that "this very crisis of conscience is a revelatory symptom."[70] As an image culture fragments into more and more images, these fragments are asking us to provide the narratives and frameworks of interpretive meanings. Such frameworks are, in reality, theological frameworks, even those that don't overtly point to God. They invite questions. What do these images mean? What are we to do in response to these images? What does it mean to be human in today's world? These are the questions of the soul in crisis.

In the face of this need for a framework, the church is faced with a missiological question: In what ways can the church create a framework for the fractured images of our culture? Such questions turn crisis into a gift. They allow the human imagination to make links and seek new possibilities.

Contemporary philosopher Slavoj Zizek calls this a "surplus." As each person processes images, they are left with the gift of a "creative surplus."[71] Thus processing images becomes the gift of creative play. In what ways can the church encourage this play, and thus encourage the search for meaning?

The answer will lie in our willingness to be creative in our understanding of ministry, worship, and community. A key mission task of the church today is to be a playful space, providing the images, the spiritual "colored pencils," and the space for people to make connections between God, themselves, others, and God's world.

Practices of creative play

How to download creativity? At the risk of limiting your creativity, but knowing that there is nothing new under the sun, try the following recipes for nurturing creativity, many of which have been "cooked" in the Graceway kitchen.

1. Ask the Creative Spirit of God to be present.
2. Take a good look at the interior of your worship space, whether home or hall, church or café. How can you add images and creatively "play" with the environment?
3. Run storytelling evenings. Invite people to tell the story of something on them—rings, piercings, belts. Where did these symbols come from? What do they tell others about you?
4. Hand out random objects to anyone who speaks or teaches in your community. Invite these people to use their object in their speaking or teaching at some point during the coming year.
5. Weave as many different voices as you can into your expressions of church life. Look at art from a different ethnic community. Let a child read Scripture. Ask a single person to offer a community blessing or have an elderly person serve communion.
6. Hang artwork in your worship space and encourage artists to add their work as well.
7. Incorporate the five senses with the theme of your worship, brainstorming ideas around each sense: hearing, sight, taste, touch, and smell. How would the senses play into Pentecost Sunday or the story of the Road to Emmaus?
8. Run art and theology courses. Divide your time in three. A third will be Bible teaching. A third will be learning an art technique by inviting a local artist to teach you. A third will be given to creative expressions of the Bible themes.
9. Offer an open invitation to actors and dancers who can give new life to familiar passages of Scripture through the spoken word or creative movement.

imaginary museum: The Christchurch Art Gallery hosted an audio installation by David Clegg. "The Imaginary Museum" involved places around the museum with comfortable couches, newspapers, and walkmans. Open the newspaper and you were presented with close up camera shots of various museums and art galleries around the world. Put on the headphones and you heard various museum directors describing their museums, reflecting on how light, or the color of the walls, or the placing of the doors, could shape our experiences of the artwork. By selecting among those real and imaginary elements, visitors are invited to assemble an ideal whole. This is an example of how the process of working with fragmented images leads to a surplus after the assembly of an *ideal whole*. For more, see www.imaginarymuseum.com

10. Write a book on creative worship and invite readers to use their God-given creativity to "cook" their own, unique recipes. Invite the posting of any of the creativity recipes on the open forum at www.emergentkiwi.org.nz and pass on the creativity download blessings.

11. Create a community mosaic to represent the new image created by reframing our fragmented lives.

More books

Jeremy Begbie (ed), *Beholding the Glory: Incarnation through the Arts*. Grand Rapids, Mich.: Baker Books, 2000.

William A. Dyrness, *Visual Faith. Art, Theology, and Worship in Dialogue*. Grand Rapids, Mich.: Baker Academic, 2001.

Christian Eckart, Harry Philbrick, Osvaldo Romberg (editors), *Faith: The Impact of Judeo-Christian Religion on Art in the New Millennium*. Ridgefield, Connecticut: The Aldrich Museum of Contemporary Art, 2000.

Richard Kearney, *The Wake of Imagination: Toward a Postmodern Culture*. London: Routledge, 1994.

Mitchell Stephens, *The Rise of the Image, the Fall of the Word*. New York: Oxford University Press, 1998.

Karen Stone, *Image and Spirit: Finding Meaning in Visual Art*. Minneapolis, Minn.: Augsburg Books, 2003.

More websites

www.neave.com/lab/misc/imagination.html

http://jonnybaker.blogs.com/jonnybaker/

www.sxc.hu/

www.osbd.org/article/21/

Part Three
Emerging Mission

Hi from London. I have just caught the tube to Ealing to experience Grace and meet with Jonny Baker and Steve Collins.

While Grace is known around the world for the creativity of its worship, I found their wider spiritual resourcing most challenging. Along with two other London alternative worship groups, Grace designed a portable labyrinth, complete with walkmans. The labyrinth project became a "kit" that has toured the UK and been published in the USA.

In our changing world, one small creative group can resource spirituality. It can offer its creativity as a global consumptive product, resourcing spiritual tourism. Is this Christianity Lite or deeply incarnational mission in a world that's online 24/7?

1565N

POST CARD

Postcard 5:
Spiritual Tourism

From my café table I browse a recent purchase, *Spirit at Home*. It reminds me that our current cultural air is definitely more spiritual than it once was. I see it in the crosses and statues of Jesus in Luhrmann's *Romeo and Juliet*. I experience it in the successes of *Buffy the Vampire Slayer* and the Harry Potter series. Spiritual seekers stroll the pick-and-mix supermarket of spiritual options, looking for spiritual practices. They search out ritual and mystery, hoping for relevance and cultural coherence. They want an individualism holistically connected with others.

Our craving for spirituality is built in. Being made in the image of God means you and I are created with a relational magnet that pulls us toward wholeness with the Divine. In our individuality, we are left free to nourish and nurture that relational magnetism, to adjust the settings on the weight of its pull.

David Hay has researched the spirituality of today's unchurched population. He finds that while church attendance is in free fall, reported religious experience is on the increase. Hay found that the spirituality of those outside the church is a sort of quest. A do-it-yourself theology was especially evident among people under the age of 40 who "construct a theology of their own, quite often using fragments of the Christian narrative available to them."[72]

The missional task of the church today involves respecting the magnetic urge toward God that is intrinsic in us all and finding ways to help tune the settings of those in the midst of spiritual searching so they are pointed toward God. In

on the bedside table: Jane Alexander's *Spirit at Home: How to Make your Home a Sanctuary* includes rituals to declutter and clean and re-energize your home. It causes me to ponder whether Christian spirituality has anything practical to offer.

google this: According to the latest in brain research, everyone has a spirit. For more, see Andrew Newberg, *Why God Won't Go Away.* New York: Ballantine, 2002. For fun, do a Google search for "neurotheology."

fractions: I love the description of Platform 9 3/4 in the first Harry Potter book. There is a solid brick wall between the cold logic of Platform 9 and Platform 10—but if you run at it the right way, you break through into another world: a magical, messy world of compound fractions. If logic rules the day, our world is lost. But if there is another world between the lines, a world in which a kindly headmaster can declare us safe, then there is hope. That's magic, that's spirituality. That's resurrection.
—Gerard Kelly

doing so, we must always remember that we are not initiators of faith, but partners both with people and with God.

At the same time, there is a temptation to domesticate God. Christians love to erect church walls and enjoy the Spirit in safety—on our terms. Spiritual seekers can fall into the trap of picking and choosing a feel-good theology that doesn't have anything to do with the truth of living life with God. Yet the Spirit of God in the Bible is heaven-bent on blowing away domestication. In the Old Testament, the Spirit is *ruach,* the wind of God. In the Middle East, this *ruach* is the wind that blasts grit through desert gully, spitting sand against worn rock. It is a wild, primal, and powerful wind. In the New Testament, the Spirit moves the church beyond walls, beyond the culture. It is a wind that blows beyond one's comfort zone. Always the Spirit is in the world.

Tourist spirituality

The movie *Before Sunrise* is one of my favorite romantic movies. It is the story of a North American backpacker who meets a young European student while traveling Europe by train. They share a magical 14 hours in Vienna. It perfectly captures the unexpected, unknown wonders that come about when tourism is thought of as a quest rather than a task.

For many young people, an overseas experience (OE) is an essential rite of passage. Nervous, backpacked young adults kiss even more nervous parents goodbye at airports. Armed with naiveté and money from Mom and Dad, fortified by stories of adventure and a few addresses, and fueled by promises to write, the traveler sets off. This time is not about getting a job or pursuing a degree. It is a year or two of exploring new places, new perspectives, and new experiences. This OE, this rite of passage, often becomes a form of quest and leads people to a greater appreciation of identity—their own and that of others.

at the movies: *Before Sunrise.* Starring Ethan Hawke and Julie Delpy and directed by Richard Linklater.
note to self: Make time to see the sequel, *Before Sunset,* when Hawke and Delpy meet in Paris nine years later. www. beforesunset.com

Tourism can serve as a redemptive framework for postmodern mission, in which people are "tourists" on spiritual journeys and the church operates as "tour guide," stimulating forward movement and nourishing the quest.

Movement

Anyone who has traveled knows there is no such thing as the typical tourist. Some tourists are simply *recreational*.[73] They are seeking the recreational break of a week enjoying the sunset over an abandoned beach. Give them a good book, some good food, and lots of rest, and they're happy.

Other tourists are *experiential*. They are in search of meaning in other cultures. Inquisitive and inquiring, they want to meet the locals rather than tan on a beach or stay sealed up on a pre-packaged bus trip. Exploration is an essential motivation.

Experimental tourists are seekers. They are not just exploring alternatives, they are actively hoping to find new meaning. They are on a "try-before-you-buy" search for other ways of viewing life and assessing identity.

Some experimental tourists will find what they're looking for. They could be called *existential* tourists. They have inwardly relocated to other places. When home, they are saving up money to return, sitting at their desks with their hearts in the kibbutz in Israel or at the vineyard in Italy.

All tourists are somewhere on this continuum. The characters in *Before Sunrise* might have been seeking recreation or diversion, but they found an experience that changed their view of life and the essence of who they are.

Journey

Clearly, there are parallels between tourism and spirituality. Christian formation involves the move from experiential and experimental seeker to existential relo-

in the CD player: U2, "I Still Haven't Found What I'm Looking For." *The Joshua Tree,* Island Records, 1987.

on the bedside table: Dan Eldon was a talented photojournalist. In 1992, at the age of 22, he was beaten to death while covering the civil war and famine in Somalia. His stunning art, stored in 17 journals, was turned into a book, *The Journey Is the Destination: The Journals of Dan Eldon* (Chronicle Books, 1997). The book captures his life pilgrimage, moments of beauty and despair, and the vigorous pursuit of the meaning of life. Go to daneldon.org for more on Daniel's life. Images of Daniel's art can be found at www. creativevisions.org

journeying: I think
it's important for
churches to remember,
as Graceway always
seemed to with me,
that spiritual travelers
are on a journey with
God. They're not to
be rushed along,
herded through a
numbered sequence
of steps or pushed
over a set course of
obstacles. Only the
journeyer and God
know exactly where
they are together at
any one time, and only
God knows where he
wants them to go next.
So, support but don't
push, and guide but
don't try to grab the
wheel.
—Kelli Robson

on the bedside table:
Nelson Graburn.
"Tourism: The Sacred
Journey," in *Hosts
and Guests: The
Anthropology of
Tourism*, ed. Valence
L. Smith (Philadelphia:
University of
Pennsylvania Press,
1989).

on the bedside table:
See John Drane,
*Evangelism for a New
Age: Creating Churches
for the Next Century.*
London: Marshall
Pickering, 1994, pp.
97-110.

cation to a new place of being and understanding. It is in essence a call to tour, to journey spiritually with God. It is a move away from recreation and diversion toward an inward relocation of heart and mind.

For centuries God's people have toured physically: from Abraham's sojourn into Canaan to Israel's wilderness wanderings, from the Via Dolorosa to Paul's missionary journeys, from medieval pilgrimage to the literary imagery of John Bunyan's writings. But as each of these examples proves, the journey is rarely linear.

Take the pilgrim Peter. Jesus calls Peter to follow him, but it's hard to know when Peter truly accepted the invitation. Was it when Jesus said, "Follow me"? When Peter said, "You are the Messiah"? When Jesus said "Get behind me Satan"? Was Peter a Christian when he denied Jesus, or when Jesus said, "Feed my sheep"? Perhaps it was at the point of Peter's worldview conversion in Acts 10, when he realized Christianity was bigger than his cultural upbringing. Yet he slipped back into his old racist patterns in Galatians 2. Peter is on a pilgrim journey that has few straight lines, but it is always moving him forward, toward God.

Or take the apostle Paul. We often interpret his Damascus Road experience as a dramatic conversion. Dramatic yes, but in reality it was more of a commission than a conversion. Commission for mission is certainly how Paul describes it and this is consistent with the fact that Paul is a God-fearing expert on the Old Testament. For Paul, the move was not from unawareness to awareness but from hostility to acceptance.

The stories of Peter and Paul point us toward a new understanding of the spiritual journey. With Peter, we see that the move from recreational tourist to existential tourist does not come all at once—true existential tourists don't start out that way but rather grow in their willingness to open themselves to the possibilities of other cultures, other experiences. With Paul, we see that the journey is rarely known and mapped out—God can and does intervene in surprising ways. In both cases, we see that the most meaningful tours often are those that take the traveller down uncertain paths and into unknown regions.

Following the signposts

The metaphor of spiritual tourism doesn't discount the need for decision-making points along the way; a tourist left to his own devices can become hopelessly lost. So it is the role of the church, of those of us on the journey now, to create signposts that allow the traveler to get oriented. In doing so, however, we need to be cautious of the "in" and "out" mentality that can cripple the church. The signposts we create are not meant to exclude some from the journey but to guide all who wish to walk.

Kelli is a woman who found faith through Graceway. I asked her what helped her move from timid experimental tourist to existential convert. She told me she experienced Graceway as a listening church; a personal church; a relational church; a deep-thinking church; a multimedia church; a living, breathing church; an inclusive, accepting church; an honest, real church.

Kelli also noticed the many signposts that oriented her faith search. They included the concrete take-home reminders of worship gatherings, such as images of Jesus and Advent stones. They included attention to the artifacts of her world—popular music and nature, the community website in which she could process faith, and individual people who listened to her growth pains.

The mission of the church is to act as a resource for spiritual tourists. The church must search for ways to move people from *recreation* to *experimentation* to *existential* relocation into the kingdom of God. We can do that by acting as tour guides on the spiritual journey.

The guide can make or break the tourist's journey. The tour guide can deepen knowledge, explain local custom, and ensure a safe space in which to explore

tourism: This is a helpful metaphor and one that sparks all kinds of possible imaginative responses. Tourists will only stop off at an attraction if it is interesting to them—if it is, in fact, attractive. Should we be surprised that so many have not "stopped off" at our churches, since we have made little or no effort to be attractive? But what will convince pilgrims that this Jesus experience is not just another attraction along the way? If conversion is a journey and discipleship is an invitation to tour, will those we welcome through the front door cheerfully be leaving through the back door? I don't ask in order to dismiss the tourist metaphor, but because I think we need to reflect long and hard about what else we do besides offering "Jesus Tours." Tourism, in fact, mitigates against longevity and commitment, as you'll know if you've ever tried to stay on at your paradise hotel after your allotted two weeks. What are the metaphors of longevity, of rootedness and "staying-put" that can shape this other aspect of the church's task?
—Gerard Kelly

crossing guards:
A new or non-believer may have to make a number of intrepid crossings before they step inside your church. They may have used up most of their courage just convincing themselves to call and find out when you meet, or telling someone at home, "Yes, I am really going to go to church." They may have driven white-knuckled to your church parking lot and sat in the car for five minutes. Taking on, or even trying on, a completely new understanding of the entire universe is scary! So be patient and be gentle, even if no bridge but attendance is crossed for quite some time.
—Kelli Robson

global spiritual places: Iona, Holy Island of Lindisfarne, Whitby, Mull of Kintyre, Taize, Jamaica, Azusa Street.
—John and Olive Drane

and experience. The tour guide can create an invitation for continuing the journey or shut down the desire to return. An effective guide has an intuitive sense of what the tourist needs and is ready for. This tour guide provides opportunities for exploration beyond what's expected and offers resources for deepening the impact of the journey.

I realize this sounds like a consumeristic understanding of the church, that I'm suggesting we tread carefully with our "tourists" and let them set the agenda for their own spiritual formation. But rather than let our defenses spring up, consider the ways in which the practices of the church can become places of respite and revelation for those moving toward an existential, life-altering faith.

Spiritual tourism at gathered worship

One year for Holy Week, Graceway provided "a smorgasbord space" in which to celebrate the events leading up to Easter. We rented a room in the local community hall and created an environment where visitors could experience the sights, smells, and sounds of the Passion in customized ways. A single artistic image of Easter was projected on the wall. White cloth draped the walls, while groups of candles provided the only light and ambient music the only sound. We also laid out a number of options to help people navigate the space, including water for washing hands as a symbolic cleansing ritual, and a written guide with a contemplative prayer and other suggested meditations. A portion of Scripture was read aloud every fifteen minutes.

These are familiar resources—Scripture, music, ritual, and image—used in new ways. People were free to come and go. They chose when to use the resources, when to listen to Scripture, when to meditate on the Easter image, when to seek forgiveness through cleansing, when to leave. This approach takes nothing away from the power of the gospel, but rather allows spiritual tourists to respond to that power in their own time and way.

Lev Manovich is a new media sage. He argues that contemporary culture has moved from objective space to what he calls *navigable space*. Navigable space is part of the postmodern shift and describes the way each of us now experiences time, space, and motion in new ways. The Internet is a great example. As I click my way, link by link, through the Internet —Refresh and Favorites, Forward and Back—I experience the instantaneous collapse of time and space.

Browsing the Internet is a navigable experience of random, rather than sequential, acts. The linear nature of logical argument is broken by hyperlinks. Linear time is broken by the 24/7 nature of the Web world. We can read the everyday lives of people who are already in tomorrow. While we sleep, people browse our sites. The Internet allows us to navigate in new ways through time and space.

Cityside Baptist Church provides a Wednesday night service of navigable space. It allows visitors to navigate the experience with the church as tour guide. There is live music, a constantly changing array of projected images, and spaces for confession, praise, and intercessory prayer. Visitors move through these stations at their own pace, spending as long as they like at each station. After all, each person comes with differing needs. Those burdened to pray have time to pray. Those with much to confess have the space to seek cleansing. Live music and visuals ensure a sense of the holy. This service concludes with 15 minutes of liturgical prayer, blending individual reflection with the corporate act.

The church becomes a provider of spiritual images, symbols, music, and resources. While location is fixed, the church is cooperating with the way our contemporary culture accesses information and experience and reflects on them. The church is allowing tourists to navigate their way through the rich resources of the Christian tradition.

Alan Hirsh and Mike Frost have developed the term "proximity spaces." These are places outside the church in which Christians can develop relationships with

on the bedside table: Michael Frost and Alan Hirsh, *The Shape of Things to Come: Innovation and Mission for the 21st-Century Church*. Peabody, MA: Hendrickson, 2003.

spiritual tourists. Having freed worship to be navigable space, it is then a logical step for the church, acting as tour guide, to provide resources in proximity spaces.

A proximity space could be a café that includes a "Holy Week space" like the one we created at Graceway. Images, rituals, and written readings allow visitors to come and sit with Scripture at their pace. Proximity space could look like our outdoor peace service organized in response to the war in Iraq. For two nights we gathered in a public space at the center of our local community to read Scripture, listen to U2's "Peace on Earth," [74] light candles, and take olive branches as a reminder that peace can start in our homes. This was not meant to be a political statement but to provide a proximity space for people to pray for all those affected by war.[75] Passersby stopped and lit candles. Three months later, one visitor took a next step and attended our worshipping community.

There is an essential theological principle at stake here. The church is a participator with the unseen wind of the Spirit of God. There is a trust that people have an innate spirituality that moves them on a quest for God.

These examples focus on what happens within corporate worship. But what happens as people move from gathered worship to their weekly lifestyles?

The experiences of navigable space

We live in an experience economy. According to business consultants B. Joseph Pine II and James H. Gilmore, culture has shifted from a production economy to a consumptive experience economy.[76] The economic focus now includes not only goods and services, but also experiencing those goods and services.

When you visit an art gallery, for example, your visit is most likely shaped by someone else. The gallery will have considered not just the art, but the color of the walls, the lighting in the room, the positioning of the art, and the information you have been given. All of

worship plans: Before you turn people loose, make sure they have at least some guidance. Plan most services so that if someone turns up off the street who has never been to your, or any, church before, they'll be comfortable. They should know what to do. And on the flip side, I think it's a good idea to check out what the service plan is before inviting a friend who's a new or non-believer.
—Kelli Robson

the economy of faith: For those of you uneasy with metaphors of economy in framing worship, it is worth reading through to the end of Pine and Gilmore's book, *The Experience Economy: Work is Theatre and Every Business a Stage.* (Harvard Business School Press, Boston, Mass., 1999.) They conclude by arguing that experiences must lead to transformation and honoring Jesus as the master of human transformation.

this will have been carefully considered to enhance your experience of the art.

And so we need to consider the possibilities of providing memorable experiences. In an interactive culture that values choice, the church as tour guide can serve by offering interactive experiences. Essential to this are multisensory environments that encourage lingering, provide ways for guests to participate, and encourage the attainment of skills and knowledge through exploration.

Experiences come in four shapes. They can entertain, educate, allow escape, or be an esthetic backdrop. Pine and Gilmore view these as four quadrants of a grid, titled (from the top left) entertainment, educational, escapist, and esthetic. They then challenge the experience provider to work toward a fully orbed experience. "When all four realms abide within a single setting, then and only then does *plain space* become a *distinctive place* for staging an experience."[77] Yes, tourists can find escape. Yes, they can be entertained. But the goal is the shift to a distinctive place and the crafting of experiences in all four areas.

This is done by providing inviting experiences and pathways for people to move from being passive to active participants. We do that by providing navigable space that allows tourists to move from experiential to experimental "seekers" to existential converts.

A conscious provision of impressions is essential to the creation of navigable space. Pine and Gilmore write, "The experience must be rendered with indelible impressions. Impressions are the 'takeaways' of the experience."[78] The power of this is in that one word—"takeaway." How can we help people take away our worship, and so keep working on their God experiences in the days and weeks that follow?

surfing in cyberspace: *The "Kama Sutra" of an Emerging Church: Positioning Ourselves to Engage the Senses* **by Paul Fromont. www.the-next-wave. org/stories/storyReader$145**

Absorption	
ENTERTAINMENT	**EDUCATIONAL**
Passive participation	Active participation
ESTHETIC	**ESCAPIST**
	Immersion

I designed a worship experience for our Good Friday service at Graceway. In the middle of the room was a plain white sheet. The worship focused around the (educational) act of reading the entire Easter narrative. During this lengthy engagement with Scripture, people were invited at any time to respond, to navigate through this space by expressing how they felt about what they were hearing. This response involved pulling on plastic gloves, receiving thick dollops of paint on their palms, and then smearing the paint on the white sheet. Corporately, we were left with a visual expression of pain and love, which contrasted with the white environment we would create on Easter Sunday.

As each individual finished, the worship leader peeled off the gloves. The glove, with the leftover paint caught inside, was pressed onto the palm of each participant with the words "Go, you are stained no more." Paint covered the glove, but the person's palm remained clean. This impression of cleansing is at the heart of Easter Friday and became the takeaway.

One woman told of how she struggled to wash her hands all through the Easter weekend. Every washing brought back memories and returned her to the heart of the Easter story. I use this story to illustrate experience and impression, and the way they become takeaway, which can nourish people in their spiritual quest beyond the worship service.

The plain white sheet and the use of paint provided an *esthetic* backdrop. The removal of the glove offered the chance to *escape* from one's feelings of being stained. I did not want to create *entertainment* in a diversionary sense, but I did want to use Scripture and response to draw people into the story and thus to *educate* them both about what happened historically at Easter and the freedom offered us today.

This then becomes a missionary challenge. How do our worship spaces impress? How are we helping people to process beyond Sunday? What spiritual takeaway are we providing, so that our neighbors and friends might move from escape to gospel education, from entertainment to gospel content? How can these insights shape our worship?

The routines of navigable space

I've focused on how spiritual tourists can be nourished in their spirituality. But we also need to consider the value of providing navigable space for the spiritual development and discipleship of the tour guides who create it.

One of the approaches to emerging church worship is what I call the routines of navigable space. Rather than one worship leader, the worship service is built around a set of segments—call to worship, praise, confession, worship, message, community time, intercession, and benediction.[80] Different community members are given responsibility for each segment, along with the freedom to shape and craft their segment as they like. This shaping is not the reading or enacting of something someone else has prepared for them. It gives each leader the creative freedom to navigate and craft their own worship segment.

Such an opportunity will raise a whole raft of questions for the segment leaders, and in so doing become a rich tool of spiritual formation. We live in a new cultural context. Confession and community time take on new meaning. The chaos of life will shape the ways in which praise is expressed from week to week. The life-quest of the segment leader will play into the way she crafts her piece of the whole. In this fertile seedbed comes the invitation to reflect much more deeply on faith and life.

Thus the segment leaders are allowed navigable space to explore their faith and spirituality. They are asked to reflect on their experiences as tourists on a spiritual journey. The tourist has now become the tour guide. This is a shift from consumption to community as the tourist-turned-segment leader offers spiritual resources to other visiting tourists. Christian faith becomes visible, embodied, and shared from one tourist to another. We are faced with the emergence of mission,

participation: When it's my turn to lead a segment, it's my experience that in the time leading up to that Sunday—whether I need to or I want to or I choose to—I end up thinking about God more and some aspect as part of the preparation for participating. So that's part of the reason I enjoy being on the roster, because of my participation in that service.
—Emerging church participant

the life of Christ made available to the world in the lives of Christ's body, the church.

Spiritual tourism beyond gathered worship

Walter Brueggemann describes the task of mission in a postmodern world as one of funding, of providing the bits and pieces out of which a new world can be imagined. The emergent church needs to see itself as "funding" tourists, providing a passage that is deep and wide enough to enable postmodern people to navigate their way to God.

Sourcing tourism through the provision of spiritual resources can be a key mission task of the emerging church. This builds on some of the current worshipping practices of the emerging church. It invites a move beyond gathered worship to consider how the church can be missionary, offering its spirituality resources as spiritual product to a spiritually hungry world without expecting the crossing of a threshold of a church door. Let me give a few practical examples.

Souvenirs. Most tourists bring home souvenirs. When I talk of souvenirs, I am not thinking of kitsch. I'm thinking of photographs, personal mementos, shopping bags, and those soaps, shampoos, and sewing kits from hotel rooms. These are souvenirs. When the tourist returns home, the handling of these takeaway souvenirs rekindles memories. The emerging church asks itself what kind of physical souvenirs we can send home with those who journey with us.

For the last few years, churches like Graceway and Cityside have used art as part of the Advent experience in the Sundays leading up to Christmas. Each Sunday, a different piece of art was introduced for reflection. The art pieces were printed on postcards and distributed. Attendees could take them home as a spiritual memento for the week and perhaps return to the reflections of Sunday's experience. They served as a spiritual takeaway, a souvenir to hang on the fridge door.

At this juncture, the souvenirs become missionary. Everyone remotely connected with the church can

on the bedside table: Walter Brueggemann, *Texts under Negotiation. The Bible and Postmodern Imaginatio,* Minneapolis: Fortress Press, 1993, 20.

takaway: I once preached at an Advent service in Kilwinning Abbey. The children sprayed fir cones silver and typed labels with the words, "As this cone opened up in the sunshine, may your life open to God this Advent." The labels and the cones were attached with red ribbon, and one given to each person. This was something to take home and put on their Christmas tree—spirituality2go. For the full story, see my book, *Clowns, Storytellers, Disciples.*
—Olive Drane

be sent a pack of four postcards. The church as tour guide is now offering spirituality to people both gathered and scattered. The e-mails and letters of gratitude flow in.

When churches start adding physical souvenirs, people have access to spiritual resources without having to open a church door. A theological stake has been driven into the ground. The church has recognized that people are at different places in their spiritual journeys. The church is loving people enough to go into the "highways and byways," trusting the wind of the Spirit to do its work in people's lives.

Spirituality2go. I was sent a gift this week. It was a hardback, hand-crafted blank journal. On the front was pasted an icon, the number 14, and a hand-drawn title: "Pilgrim Journal." On the inside front cover was this explanation: "This Pilgrim Journal project is an independent, privately funded attempt to follow journals through their travels. The goal is to provide interaction and sharing of creativity in relation to life, God, and faith."

The first page provided some stimulus in the form of image and text. The blank pages were an invitation for me to document my spirituality, to journal for five days—thoughts, ideas, drawings, photos, recipes, reflections. I was invited to journal with my friends. Then I was to mail it on to someone else.

This is a step beyond physical souvenirs for those in churches or on the fringes of churches. This is "spirituality2go," a missional commitment to offer spiritual fragments to those questing, to those who, in the words of David Hay, are "rethinking, construct[ing] a theology of their own, quite often using fragments of the Christian narrative." This is a willingness to cast our bread upon the waters and serve a generation of people whose experience of life demands

postcards: An e-mail came today from a woman in another country who somehow got hold of a set of Advent postcards. "Amidst all the bustle and chaos, I've kept before me those images from the Advent in art series, and occasionally the power of those still-powerful images has made me gasp at the magnitude of what happened when a vulnerable young girl gave birth to a baby." Another woman, who hasn't been near a church for a decade, recently bought two copies and gave them to non-Christian friends.
—Mark Pierson

some assembly required: The biggest mistake of the Christian churches of late modernity was to give converts a map of the "Christian World," with instructions for survival and enjoyment. But the landscapes in which faith must be proved are not the landscapes of the church but of the world. This is why exile is a better metaphor for Christianity than Holy Land: we are sent out as resident aliens to every corner of the culture. Whatever spirituality we offer must be a spirituality2go. It must be portable, lightweight, easily assembled at home, viable and usable in all the many spaces offered to us. The church has for years dealt in beliefs. In recent decades it has learned again to deal in experiences. It has largely failed, and is failing, to deal in resources.
—Gerard Kelly

24/7, instant, online access. The tour guide church must figure out what it means for the church to produce spirituality2go, the "Lonely Planet" guides, the CDs, DVDs, and websites that allow tourists to browse our spirituality.

Our church was committed to connecting with our community. We ran a number of art exhibitions working with the local artists, dialoging through art about the spirituality of Christmas. It was a rich conversation. We put together a group for young mothers in the community where they could meet and talk and offer support to one another. We were building some networks in our community.

spirituality exercise: Take some soil into your hand and think about what needs to grow in your life.

As a church we met regularly and invited people in the community to worship with us. We hoped that through relationships people might journey with us into church. It's a common way to do evangelism.

We stood back and noticed something. All our community events were pointing back to the church service. "Come to our program and by-the-way-here-is-a-special-Mother's-Day-service-you-should-attend." The hidden message was that the only way to access spirituality at Graceway was one hour on Sunday morning.

Using the tourist image, we were saying to any spiritually searching tourists that the best way to get more spirituality was to visit our shop. But good luck in catching us, because we are actually open only one hour each week.

As a course correction, we commissioned the design of another set of spirituality postcards, each with a Bible verse, a spiritual quote, and a spiritual exercise. Working with this notion of tourism, we tried to design the spiritual exercises for anyone on a spiritual quest, whether experimental or existential. The cards linked to our website, which had an exegesis of the Bible verse and more spiritual resources and exercises. We then placed these postcards in cafés all around our city. We were taking the resources from our Sunday worshipping heart and offering them 24/7—in postcards, on the Web, as an in-hand tour guide.

As a result we opened up new missionary terrain. We were interviewed on student radio. We talked with a person fresh from a Tibetan Buddhist monastery. We had phone calls from people in other cities asking for more postcards. The spiritual tourist metaphor led to the creation of a rich missional resource.

The metaphor of church as spiritual tour guide invites the church to face the missionary task of funding spiritual pilgrims, of providing spiritual resources to nourish the navigable space of spiritual tourists. It is time to partner with the Spirit of God in our wider world, rather than simply inviting people to come to us.

the best thing about cybermonks: . . . is that I can crash the monastery. I can visit, I can see, I can leave a mark. And I can do that any time I like.
—Kelli Robson

Cybermonks. Internet use is a form of tourism. Cybertourists search for identity in an arena so vast it acts as a level playing field in which all have equal access to its riches. Traveling in cyberland involves a form of pilgrimage, including the ritual of leaving home (dialing up) to wander an interconnected world of conversation and spiritual resources, before returning home by logging off.

In this world, the emerging church needs cybermonks to act as spiritual guides. They blog their stories with image, narrative, and experience. They design websites to provide spiritual resources online. This is not a modern "come to us because we have a great worship service." This is a postmodern "here are our spiritual resources, feel free to try-before-you-buy." The cybermonk is a new missionary calling.

Simon Jenkins and Bruce Stanley are cybermonks who developed www.rejesus.co.uk/.[81] Two years in development, it offers information about Jesus and his life, downloads of the Gospels, and contemporary expressions of faith including real-life stories, poems, and photographs. There are places to pray online, to explore Celtic spirituality, and to light a candle electronically as an act of prayer. There is even an online labyrinth that offers a journey with music, meditation, and suggestions for symbolic action or ritual. The site encourages community interaction through community boards, online quizzes, and a place to ask hard questions. The aim is to reach spiritual tourists—people with little previous knowledge of Christianity—and to encourage them to take next steps.

Spiritual tourism: Sold out or selling out?

Your theological antennae may be twitching, uneasy with the links between tourism and consumerism. And surely the church today is consumptive enough without suggesting we encourage mission as loading up tourists with spiritual product. In my defense, let me make two practical comments, followed by one theological comment.

First, we need to be fair to tourists. They all come from different places and travel for different reasons. Yes, some are consumptive. But not all. And none need remain so. As I've already suggested, it's the poor tour guide who leaves a tourist less educated. It's up to the church to ensure that its spiritual product educates and that our navigable space is deep enough to honor the Christ who died for the entire cosmos. There is no reason why spirituality2go can't be deeply spiritual—take up your cross and follow—rather than Christianity Lite, complete with artificial sweetener and chocolate frosting.

Second, let's give people (including ourselves) credit. In Postcard 2, I introduced the work of French Jesuit Michel de Certeau. His research showed how we all "make do." We all DJ, taking the information we are given, at times to amplify culture, at times to subvert culture, at times to juxtapose culture. This is the power of consumption.

We've all looked out the window as the preacher preached and made our own life application. Consumerism is simply the way we live and move and have our being. It need not drive us to a loss of soul; people are adaptive, re-creative creatures.

From a theological standpoint, if we hold that all people have a spirituality, spiritual tourism is not an act of consumption, but an alignment with a heart that

11 commandments of a healthy spirituality of consumption:
Consume No Logo.
Consume Ad Busters.
Consume no meat.
Consume fair trade.
Consume using your own shopping bags.
Consume recyclable packaging.
Consume second hand clothing.
Consume at sales.
Consume no pirated software.
Consume no CFCs.
Consume the body of Jesus.

is restless until it has found its home in God. The church as tour guide is thus a creative act of partnership with the stirrings of the Spirit of God. It is a sharing of the mission of Jesus, who loved culture so much that his heart beat with Jewish blood, he loved God in a Jewish way, and his feet navigated their way through a Jewish culture. Because Jesus was alive, local, and navigating God in one culture, God can be alive, local, and navigated in other cultures. To share in the mission of Jesus is to ask how Jesus' heart can beat with postmodern blood and how people can be called to love and follow Jesus in a postmodern way. The offering of real faith, the integrity of the tour guides, the sharing of experiences that are entertainment, escapist, esthetic, and educational will ensure the movement from experiential or experimental seekers to radically committed existential converts of Jesus Christ.

listen in: But when he, the Spirit of truth, comes, he will guide you into all truth. He will not speak on his own; he will speak only what he hears, and he will tell you what is yet to come. —John 16:13

More books

Bruce Demarest, *Soulguide: Following Jesus as Spiritual Director*, Colorado Springs, Colo.: NavPress, 2003.

Michael Grimshaw, "Tourist, Traveler, or Exile: Redefining the Theological Endeavour." *Journal of Religion* 81, 2, (April 2001) pp. 249-270.

B. Joseph Pine II and James H. Gilmore. *The Experience Economy: Work is Theatre and Every Business a Stage.* Boston: Harvard Business School Press, 1999.

More websites

www.damah.com

www.yfc.co.uk/labyrinth/online.html

Thomas M. Beaudoin. "After Purity: Contesting Theocapitalism." Located at www.ptsem.edu/iym/downloads/lectures_01/AFTERPUR.PDF

Hi again. I'm now in North America.

The more I travel, the more I realize there are some interesting church shapes emerging. Groups like Vineyard Central and Vine & Branches Christian Community (I did not have time for personal experience, so "listened" at www.vbcc.net and at www.vineyardcentral.com.) are using community as their emerging church building block.

These communities are in fact groups of communities on a journey that includes no buildings, no paid staff, and no Sunday morning service. Instead there are groups of communities; some actually live together, others meet weekly at different times and in different places.

What resources exist to help the emerging church build community?

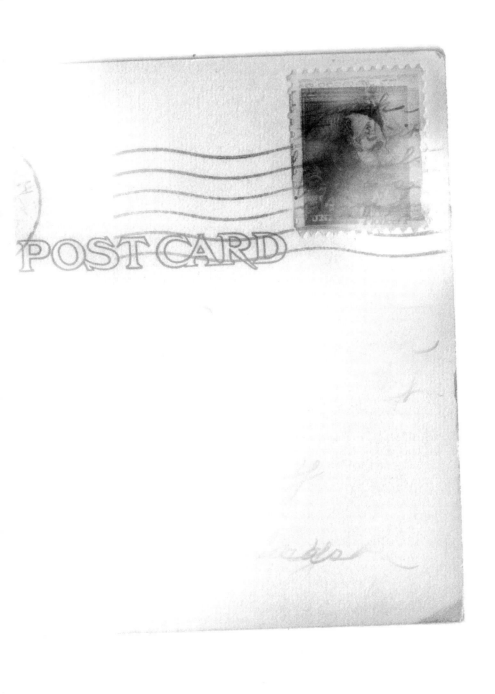

POST CARD

Postcard 6:
Redemptive Portals

Let me tell you a story of redemption in community. "I saw you holding hands," the young man said to me, looking slightly embarrassed. Brian had grown up Catholic, but had spent his adulthood a long way from those religious roots.

The emerging church I was planting hoped to find redemption in community. We met over a meal. We had a barstool—a literal barstool—where we gave space for people to share their stories each week. We wanted to create a place in which people could share their lives, and in so doing, find life.

One Sunday night, as he walked past the glass doors of the community hall where we met, Brian saw us holding hands. Drawn by us holding hands and the sense of community he observed, Brian returned the next week. "I saw a community I could participate in," he told us. Brian was a seeker who sought touch in community. He had realized that God has a body and that Christian faith is a contact sport. Modernity has emphasized rationality. In so doing, we have run the risk of stripping the mind from the body and of losing sight of Jesus, who invited the disciple Peter to follow him in a discipling community long before Peter could rationally verbalize his faith (Matthew 4:18-20, 16:16).

I've been told that seekers seek God in anonymity. Yet contemporary cultural observers are suggesting that, like Brian, seekers are seeking community. As I've said, Douglas Coupland's landmark novel, *Generation X*, follows three young people who "came to the desert—to tell stories and to make [their] own lives worthwhile tales in the process."[83] The desert is a place of retreat. In Coupland's story, it is a place to withdraw from the clean, shiny surfaces of our material world. In the desert comes the quest, the finding of meaning.

redemption: n. the purchase back of something that had been lost.[82]

redemptive practices: safe space, hospitality, shared lives, finding Christ in the stranger, welcoming diversity, embracing difference.

in the CD player: U2, "The First Time," *Zooropa*, Polygram International Music Publishing, 1993.

reading Coupland: I stood up and was considering this drop of blood when a pair of small fat arms grabbed around my waist, fat arms bearing fat dirty hands tipped with cracked fingernails. It was one of the mentally retarded teenagers, a girl in a sky blue calico dress, trying to pull my head down to her level. I could see her long, streaky, fine blond hair from my height, and she was drooling somewhat as she said, *urrd*, meaning bird, several times.

I bowed down on my knees again before her while she inspected my talon cut, hitting it gently with an optimistic and healing staccato caress—it was the faith-healing gesture of a child consoling a doll that has been dropped.

Then, from behind me I felt another pair of hands as one of her friends joined in. Then another pair. Suddenly I was dog-piled by an instant family, in their adoring, healing, uncritical embrace, each member wanting to show their affection more than the other. They began to hug me—too hard—as though I were a doll, unaware of the strength they exerted. I was being winded— crushed—pinched and trampled.

The man with the beard came over to yank them away. But how could I explain to him, this well-intentioned gentleman, that this discomfort, no this *pain*, I was experiencing was no problem at all, that in fact, this crush of love was unlike anything I had ever known.

—Douglas Coupland, *Generation X*, 1st ed, 178-179.

While our assumption is that the desert symbolizes loneliness and separation, for Coupland meaning is found not in isolation but as life stories are shared in this place apart. In community comes redemption. Lives become worthwhile tales in the sharing of stories. Communal meaning replaces individualized materialism. Three spiritual tourists notify us that community is a redemptive place in contemporary society.

Generation X ends with a scene in which human contact and care become vehicles for unconditional acceptance. Andy, who starts the book withdrawing from society, finishes the book experiencing a healing crush of love. This experience of self-giving love occurs in community and is received through human arms. Redemption is a contact sport.

For Brian, belonging to a community preceded belief. Brian joined the church roster and brought food for the community meal before he owned faith for himself. Like the disciple Peter, Brian was prepared to participate in a community before he was clear about his belief in Jesus.

For their book, *Gen X Religion*, Richard W. Flory and Donald E. Miller surveyed religious practices among Gen-X groups in California. They concluded that an experience like Brian's is not unique. For Gen-Xers, "personal narrative is validated only through incorporating the values of the religious community into that narrative, and in effect, making the community narrative one's own."[84] The emerging generation wants to participate. As they participate, contribute to the community, and share their life stories, they find they incorporate the faith of the community into their own lives.

Once Brian found faith, he stretched his wings to participate in other ways. He led stranger took bread. Again, the gestures were vaguely familiar. *When he was at the table with them, he took bread, gave thanks, broke it, and began to give it to them. Then their eyes were opened and they recognized him, and he disappeared from their sight.*

It is telling that Jesus is revealed in an act of relationship, of community. Time and again in Luke "it is in the intimacy of fellowship that Jesus is recognized."[88] Jesus, the master preacher, exposits the Old Testament texts to little effect. But suddenly, amid an act of communal and human hospitality, God is revealed. To biblical text community must be added. To preaching, the mystery of bread broken and given must be added. Community becomes revelatory. In this story, God is redemptively present when friends are gathered.

I have always been fascinated by a painting of the Emmaus road story. It is titled *The Moorish Kitchen Maid* and was painted by Diego Rodrigues de Silva y Velazquez. In the foreground and dominant is the kitchen maid, who is preparing dinner. In the top right, and pushed to the background, are the two disciples and Jesus, gathered around table and in community. The maid's head is slightly turned toward the table in an attentive, listening pose. It suggests that as Christ is revealed in community, others are drawn in.

The painting raises the imaginative possibility that the revelation of Christ in community has a missional attraction that draws the bystander and wayfarer in. Redemptive community is missional. It draws in the fringes.

The artistic dreams of Velazquez warn us against making community our contemporary idol. It has been said that if you seek community you will not find it, but if you seek people, you will find community. Just as a website serves as a starting point for accessing other online destinations or activities, the point of redemptive community is not community. The point is to send you somewhere, to reveal the body of God in the world that God loves.

the barstool time. He preached his first sermon. He saw his sister, Anne Marie, come to faith. The up-front performance of a distant preacher seems strangely removed from the crush of love and the telling of stories that turn lives into worthwhile tales. Community can be fleshed out in a number of ways, in the home-church gathered in a living room, on the barstool from which life's experiences are shared, or in the sacrament of eating. Don't let the form obscure the redemptive spirituality.

on the bedside
Pete Ward, *Liq*
Church. Hendri
Paternoster, 2(

The Emmaus road

Stories have many meanings. Consider the story of Jesus appearing on the road to Emmaus.

The husband and wife walked home.[85] They were gutted. Their dreams lay shattered in front of them. Each step away from Jerusalem was like a step over cut glass. Their friend was dead, brutally flogged and then cruelly nailed to a tree.

Heads down, eyes red, they nearly collided with a fellow walker. It turned out to be an uncomfortable collision. The walker was out of touch, unaware of breaking news from Jerusalem, the latest political infighting, the recent torture and murder. When they tearfully told him of the death of their best friend, he refused a listening ear. He proceeded to preach, piling up verse after verse, book after book, upon their bowed heads.

The talk did not match the husband and wife's reality. The gap between their experience and the stranger's words, words, and more words led to some inner conflict, some serious heart burn.[86] Wearily they trudged on. They reached their village home. Their fellow villagers waited, arms folded, suspicious of the stranger.[87] Silently the couple faced the silence of their home village crowd.

Yet their dead friend had preached hospitality. The stranger must be welcomed. Wearily, still hurting, the couple insisted the stranger stay. A loaf of bread was found and the pungent aroma of their local wine filled the room.

The stranger sat. The setting seemed familiar. The couple glanced at each other. Unexpectedly, the

It is time to take redemptive community seriously. If God is in the world, then God is at work in people's lives. Sadly, at times the church is the last place to find the story of God in community. Often the church employs one trained person to tell the story and the rest of the "community" is relegated to a position of passive attendance. Unless considerable pastoral care and community development skills are in place, one person's way of finding meaning is heard over and over again while other ideas are ignored or given secondary status.

As we birthed Graceway, we committed ourselves to finding God in community. We talked about all the places where community is found and where the spiritual journey takes place—the table at the coffee house, the sofa in the living room, the barstool at the local pub. This idea of common settings as places of sharing deconstructed the idea of the authoritative spiritual expert who is only accessed at certain times and in certain places. It opened us up to the possibilities of finding God through and in one another.

A number of years later I was asked to share Graceway's story with a group in Scotland. I spoke about a number of things, including the table, sofa, and barstool.

When I finished speaking, the first question was, "How do you control the barstool?" "There is no control," I replied. And that's the point: We can't control the ways in which God works in us and through us. We can't control where and when God speaks. I have often found that the work God does at the barstool is extraordinary. It would be foolish to get in the way.

This concern about authority in community is based in the fear that the barstool, and all that it entails, might lead to human subjectivity and emotion. However Christianity is uniquely placed in response to this concern.

The revelation of God in community is undergirded by the Christian understanding of God, active as the three persons of the Trinity. The church-as-community is enlivened by the Spirit of God and shaped to

letting go: What else in our worship should we trust to the "God of community"? What about preaching, public prayer, confession, leadership, all of the order of worship?
—Mark Pierson

the body of Christ: The Spirit appropriates this narrative in creating a new community in the present—the fellowship of disciples who take their identity from the narrative of Jesus. By looking to the biblical story as constituting our identity, we become the contemporary embodiment of Jesus' narrative, and, hence, we are indeed "the body of Christ."
—Stanley Grenz and John E. Franke, *Beyond Foundationalism: Shaping Theology in a Postmodern Context.* Louisville, Kentucky: Westminster John Knox Press, 2000, p. 80.

consuming with the body of Christ: Grab the best chef you know. Invite your friends to a spiritual experience called "eating your way through Luke."
• Levi's banquet (Luke 5): bean and meat casserole
• Disciples eating corn (Luke 6): corn, roasted and served with mustard-infused butter
• Son of man, eating and drinking (Luke 7): stuffed quail
• Feeding 5000 (Luke 9): fish fried in dill
• Parable of the Rich Fool (Luke 12): deep fried locust in minted yogurt dip
• Parable of the Great banquet (Luke 14): Jewish vintage
• Zaccheus' house (Luke 19): roasted chick peas
• Last Supper (Luke 22): baking Jewish bread
• Emmaus road (Luke 24): leeks sautéed in saffron

the image of Jesus, the Body of God, in accordance with the Word of God (the Bible). Thus the (trinitarian) community of God ensures the church-as-community will have both a coherent form and continuity with the past and into the future. So Christianity need not fear that authority in community will result in human subjectivity, so long as the community recognizes the Spirit of God at work.

The body of God

In John 1, the Word is made flesh and moves into the neighborhood. This enfleshed Word forms a community, a group of people. The community embodies the redemptive love of God.

Then in John 20:21, the sending Jesus breathes on this community. They receive the Spirit and are sent, as Jesus was sent. And so the task of being disciples is to form communities that embody redemptive trinitarian love.

This planting of embodied communities is essential to the mission of God. This is a shift beyond individual salvation and individual discipleship. It is a shift to the priority of community planting, within which salvation and discipleship occur.

It is not *I*, followed by *we*. It is not the individual absorbing the lone preacher and the lone preacher's words. Instead it is the *we* that validates the *I*. It is within the community that faith is found.

Lesslie Newbigin writes that the congregation is the primary hermeneutic, the primary way of understanding, for the gospel.[89] People are the window by which a culture sees God as missiology and authority are joined. The task of the church is to live the story of the gospel, preaching not only in words, but in the actions of the community. Love is heard, but love is also felt and observed through the touch of the community. This is an outrageous challenge, one that demands a fresh vision of the Trinity. The emerging church is called to flesh out the body of God, to ground ourselves as community in neighborhoods (whether relational or geographic), to touch body and soul in order to multiply community. Being the body of God is essential to redemptive community.

Three in one

The ancient creeds declare, "We believe in one, holy, catholic and apostolic church." However, the location of this oneness is contentious: Is oneness located in the universal church, or in each particular church?

This is a daily question for the emerging church. In order to establish a redemptive community of faith in a postmodern world, do we try to change where we are, or start something new? If the youth want to innovate, do we create a space where the volume is loud, or try to blend a few fast songs in with an ancient hymn or two?

Every answer has problems. If you opt to do a start-up, then you are choosing to locate oneness in the particular. It can smack of a rugged individualism and often reeks of despising the wisdom and heritage of the past. Emerging churches that take this route are often criticized for being so individuated that there is no sense of continuity with tradition whatsoever.

Yet when churches opt for oneness with the universal church, then the majority voice wins. Nothing can change. Unique identities are at risk of being lost. Rarely do innovations or minority interests float to the surface.

This is a problem heightened in the emerging church. A Dilbert cartoon says it well.[90] Dogburt recommends "forming a separate group to pursue disruptive innovations." This suggests that separation is needed in order for innovation to occur. Must the emerging church distance itself from the universal church in order to experiment?

The dream of Dogburt is immense, "a glorious place: fully funded, amazing ambience, brilliant people,

oneness: "All churches want to be catholic, though each in its own way." —Miroslav Volf. *After Our Likeness: The Church as the Image of the Trinity.* **Grand Rapids, Michigan; Cambridge, U.K.: Eerdmans, 1998, p. 259.**

building community:
Take one barstool.
Place it in the middle
of the group. Announce
it is a place to share
the good and the bad.
Create safe space
by declaring that
whatever is shared on
the barstool will be
placed before God in
prayer.

Sit back. Relax. Enjoy
the lack of control.
If there is silence,
remember that friends
are always good
enough to sit with in
silence.

The barstool has been
part of Graceway since
we started nine years
ago. It has been a
place of laughter and
tears. It has added
layers and insights to
worship and sermons.
It has brought
cultural, spiritual, and
communal life into
our community. On
the barstool we have
seen lives become
worthwhile tales
through the telling of
stories.

free from democracy!" This is what every emerging church dreams of: gifted artists, a spiritual environment, and no more cloying politics. The cartoon concludes offering the traditionalists or modernists a *once a year tour [of] the work space and the chance to sit in the beanbag chairs.*

This is the conundrum of oneness. Thankfully, the Trinity supplies the resources to allow one, holy, catholic and apostolic church to be innovative in mission in Luhrmann's world.

God as Trinity presents us with a relational understanding of God. If this is applied to the church, then the one, holy, catholic and apostolic church is understood as communal and relational. So in Matthew 18:20, the identity of the church is located as communal and relational and redemptive. "For where two or three are gathered in my name, I am among them." As on the Emmaus road, Jesus is relationally present in community. To get theological, church is "a present participation in the trinitarian *communion* through faith in Jesus Christ [that] anticipates in history the eschatological communion of the church with the triune God."[91]

The emerging church meets in a number of ways: around cafés, amid art installations, via the Internet. But whether it is the aroma of coffee, the glow of TV screens, or the hum of computer monitors, these connections are an embodied expression of the shared love of God.

This means several things.

The church rejects individualism. It is not that the emerging church decides to be the church, or that I decide to join an emerging church. Rather, if the church is the body of Christ, then our involvement is a participation in the life of this gathered community.

The ancient church described the Trinity as a *perichoresis*, the divine dance of God. It is an intensely communal and relational image. The love of God dances. Father, Son, Spirit/Creator, Redeemer, Sustainer are one in shared love.

The Spirit of God is at work in the world, ushering us into the *perichoretic* dance of God. God draws us into relationships. Our involvement is a response to God's involvement.

The church leaks love. The application of "two or three are gathered in my name" needs care. A gathered model of church often places a circle around the members. It can carry the scent of exclusivity.

A good doctrine of the Trinity views God as defined in relationships. Thus when we draw a circle around the Trinity, it is always a dotted circle to indicate that the God of the Trinity leaks love. And it includes the Trinity being incarnationally placed outside the dotted circle, within humanity, as a visible demonstration of leaked love.

It then needs lines drawn from people back into the Trinity, to indicate the redemptive grace of God that ushers us into the dance of God.

A relational Trinity that leaks love means the emerging body of God is also called to be a love-leaking community. This becomes the essence of holiness. It is not a separation from society but the integration of unique love within a society.

Oneness is located in relationships. If God is defined in relationships, then so is the church. We are one in our relationships with particular bodies— God, each other, and other churches.

This means it is dangerous to call yourself a church. By doing so, you must recognize any other group that would call itself a church. If you are the church, then so is every other grouping who call themselves the church. And you are linked to them in relationship. This means no emerging church—or any church—can imagine they are the Ground Zero of Christian faith.

Tradition is also relationship. Tradition is not the weight of past expectation nor the oppression of habitual behaviors. It is a relating to other churches throughout history. Other churches have sought to follow Christ in their cultures and we honor them in our attempts to do the same. Tradition is acknowledging these links to the past and learning from

three in one: The "unity of the trinitarian Persons lies in the circulation of the divine life which they fulfill in their relations to one another. Their unity does not lie in the one lordship of God; it is found in the unity of their tri-unity." —Jurgen Moltmann, *The Trinity and Kingdom of God.* London: SCM, 1981, p. 175.

where's the church? Our phraseology about church betrays us. Church is something we attend, a place we go, a religious event. Yet, increasingly, it is difficult to get the churched—let alone, the unchurched—over the threshold and into the building. Into what we call "church." That phenomenon may just be the postmodern ethos rebelling, that sense of true spirituality being, at base, the sharing of lives and stories, two elements that are sadly quite lacking in modern Christendom. In the United States, it is estimated that 30 percent of the unchurched are Christ-followers. Perhaps they are Christ-followers who have discovered their friends and neighbors. And that worship isn't limited to plastic plants and a sound system. —Sally Morgenthaler

the church: "Since the eschatological gathering of the people of God will include all these churches as its own anticipations, a local church cannot alone, in isolation from other churches, claim to be church. It must acknowledge all other churches, in time and space, as churches."
—Volf, *After Our Likeness,* p. 157.

the banquet: Our alternative worship group, UpLate, has come up against this diversity or conformity issue quite a lot, and actually revelled in the breadth of understanding and theology and perspectives within the group. I love the idea of the "gloriously diverse and vibrant . . . final kingdom banquet" I think that in UpLate we've had the merest taste of that, and it's good!
—Si Smith, UK practitioner

others in order to enrich our present. This is not an institutional understanding but a relational and contextually sensitive appreciation of the other. We are impoverished when we cut ourselves off from how other disciples of Jesus have served.

It's time to get missionary. I used to think that for the church to be apostolic meant we must faithfully look back to the apostles as founders of the church. I never considered the implications of the sheer missionary heartbeat of the apostles to the one, holy, apostolic church. The apostles not only looked back, they also threw forward the story of Jesus. They built new Jesus communities. To be apostolic is to continue the forward momentum of their work.

The Maori people of New Zealand have a phrase, *i nga ra o mua.* It means "to walk forward, looking back." The phrase urges walking into the future aware of one's roots and history. The identity of the emerging church must similarly walk forward, facing backward, out into the world while grounded in the Jesus story and embodying the Jesus narrative.

We believe in one, holy, catholic and apostolic church. Because it is founded in relationships, a redemptive community will seek enrichment from many in order to maximize the forward thrust of the Jesus story. This means the separate group formed to pursue innovations is indeed a glorious place only as it lives as a redemptive community, nourishing relationships with other groups.

The music can be loud and the innovation extraordinary. And if we keep redemptive community in the foreground, then imagine how much more gloriously diverse and vibrant the final Kingdom banquet will be, when the entire people of God gather.

More books

Stanley Grenz and John R. Franke, *Beyond Foundationalism: Shaping Theology in a Postmodern Context*. Louisville, Ky.: Westminster John Knox Press, 2000.

Sandra Pollerman, *Stories, Stories Everywhere: Good Practice for Storytellers*. Oxford: Bible Reading Fellowship, 2001.

Terry A. Veling and Thomas Groome. *Living in the Margins: Intentional Communities and the Art of Interpretation*. New York: Crossroad Publishing, 1996.

More websites

N. T. Wright, "How can the Bible be Authoritative?" can be found at http://home.hiwaay.net/~kbush/Wright_Bible_Authoritative.pdf

www.btinternet.com/~smallritual/sofa.html

HI FROM SEATTLE. I LOVED THE HOUSEBOATS AND THE CITY. I WISH I HAD BEEN ABLE TO VISIT GRACEWERKS (WWW.GRACEWERKS.ORG), AN ARTISTS' COLLECTIVE. I AM INTRIGUED BY THE WAY THEY MIX A COMMUNAL CENTER--A PLACE OF ACTIVITY AND RELATIONSHIP AND COLLECTIVE CREATIVITY--WITH MISSIONALLY FLUID NETWORKS.

ON HER BLOG (DEEPDIRT.BLOGSPOT.COM), KAREN WARD OF GRACEWERKS WRITES, "MANY OTHER [EMERGING] GROUPS ARE ON A 'CHURCH VIBE' ROUTE, OVERTLY 'PROFESSING' (GOSPEL/JESUS) WITHIN POSTMODERN AND YOUTH CULTURE.... NOWHERE IS GOD OR JESUS MENTIONED ON THE [GRACEWERKS] WEB SITE, AS A RADICAL (AND CHURCH HUMBLING) WAY OF SAYING THAT GOD'S PRESENCE 'IN, WITH, AND UNDER,' GOD'S OWN WORLD, IS NOT IN ANY WAY DEPENDENT UPON, OR LIMITED TO, OUR INVOCATION."

INTRIGUED, I WONDER HOW THE EMERGING CHURCH CAN, WITH INTEGRITY, INTERFACE COMMUNITY AND MISSION?

Post
Card

THIS SPACE FOR ADDRESS ONLY

U.S.POSTAGE

Postcard 7:
Missional Interface

Perhaps the greatest question facing the emerging church is how to integrate spiritual tourism with the notion of redemptive community. How do we create communities flexible enough to weather the constant influx of new people and ideas, yet stable enough to provide consistency for those who wish to commit themselves to those communities? How do we create communities that are open enough to welcome the tourist, yet orthodox enough to remain grounded in the triune God? How do we create communites where there is both the security of sound theology done well and the excitement of theology made new?

On the ground, the emerging church is exploring these tensions in a number of ways. The emerging church is in reality the emerging *churches,* which represent an assortment of redemptive forms: house churches, art collectives, weekly participative communities, incarnational church plants, and postmodern monasteries.

Some of these are tentative, more a draft print than a high-quality finished product. But they present some tantalizing possibilities for the future of redemptive communities. They also require some hard missiological thinking. In this chapter, I want to run a missiological ruler over these forms, using the insights of sociologist Zygmunt Bauman.

Forming community

Zygmunt Bauman uses the notion of a *liquid modernity* to describe our contemporary culture. Economically, modernity focused on the large-scale, production-oriented industrial structures. Yet today, with cell phones, laptops, and hot desks, we see many more mobile, individualized, consumption-focused modes of production.

the face of the church: It is a matter of interest to me that small participative groups are emerging in the post-Christian culture. I have a thesis, not yet fully tested, that the shape of the church in a post-Christian world will look like the face of the church in the pre-Christian world (prior to Constantine, 311 AD). The first three centuries of Christianity consisted of small house church groups that were, by all accounts, highly interactive. The same is true in China today. So it should be no surprise that the decline of the West and of the established church should be the context in which the house church emerges.
—Robert Webber

on the bedside table: Zygmunt Bauman, *Liquid Modernity.* Cambridge, Polity Press, 2000.

Because these modes change the way we earn and spend money, they also change the culture itself. Bauman argues that both economically and culturally, we have now embraced a more liquid, pick-and-mix, consumer-oriented way of living and working. Choice has taken over from institutional norms as individuals now choose, or "shop" for, an identity rather than simply accepting the identity they are given.

Bauman then extends this idea to the function of community in society. Just as individuals now choose identity, so they choose the communities to which they belong. Further, these choices are often expressions of personal identity. As in the world of Douglas Coupland, our notions of community are no longer found in a family related by blood. Instead, individuals search for communities of choice in which they can belong and make sense of their lives.

on the bedside table: Zygmunt Bauman, *Community: Seeking Safety in an Insecure World.* Cambridge: Polity Press, 2000.

Because of this choice, community takes different forms. Bauman describes two types of community. The first group are *peg communities*. These provide a focus, or peg, for the participation of disconnected spectators. A rock concert or a sports match is an example. Participants are offered a sense of being in community among a disconnected group of people.

coffee and community: We tend to go to cafés for reasons other than drinking coffee . . . we can do that at home—it's sometimes better and always cheaper. But what we can't do at home is be among strangers. Cafés are unique social spaces where people go specifically to be with others and yet be separate."
—Kapka Kassabova, *In the Company of Strangers,* Canvas, April 3-4, 2004.[93]

Ever-popular TV talk shows are a further example. They offer a public window into private lives. Such disclosure evokes a sense of intimacy and belonging, but that offer of belonging never requires engagement with other spectators. Individuals choose to "peg" and in so doing are offered an experience of community. Yet there is no expectation of shared lives. Bauman says, "Like the attractions on offer in theme parks, the bonds of [peg] communities are to be 'experienced' and to be experienced on the spot—not taken home and consumed in the humdrum routine of day after day."[92]

In contrast, *ethical communities* are built on long-term commitments. They offer a shared communal confidence because individuals have given up their rights. In return, they are offered ethical rights and responsibilities.

Examples of ethical communities are less common in society today. The rise of fundamentalism and the initial attraction toward some cult groups comes from the attractiveness of long-term, shared commitments. The 1970s saw the rise of many live-in, intentional communities. They were based on a shared commitment to the values of that community. In return they offered a safe environment. The largest New Age community in the world is based at Findhorn, in Scotland. More than 500 people live together, sharing a long-term commitment to peace, tolerance, and their vision for society.

Bauman's distinction between the development of peg and ethical communities in contemporary culture allows us to take a new look at the many incarnations of the emerging church. In the rest of the chapter, I want to evaluate a number of forms of emerging church in relation to Bauman's notions of peg and ethical community. I do this in order to provide a greater missiological focus for the emerging church.

Ethically pure: The house church

A common form of the emerging church is the house church.

Thus, among some Vineyard churches in the United States, churches are structured around the house. Buildings, paid pastoral staff, and regular Sunday morning services are rejected in favor of meetings in homes. The emphasis is on relationships and the deep sharing of lives through small groups of people meeting each week for intense fellowship. People become part of the house church through natural relationships. This is both a strength, as it promotes a relational and natural discipleship, and a weakness, as like attracts like. As with all friendship evangelism, it draws those who are already close, but not those relationally removed. There tends to be an inherent homogeneity.

A house church is a prime example of Bauman's ethical community, one based on shared ethical rights and responsibilities. It is difficult to "peg" in a house church. A house church involves stepping across the daunting threshold, that missiological crevasse called the door. Inside, the house church expects engagement with other participants and the sharing of lives. Still, the house church model raises questions about how those outside of the community can begin to intersect with these gatherings.

The methods and activities of the LivingRoom, a house church in Melbourne, Australia, suggest some answers. They meet in a home each week, sharing an evening meal, periods of prayer, reflection, teaching, discussion, and sharing. In addition to this ethical gathering, they deliberately create social occasions where friends of friends can meet. These *redemptive parties* are open, "everybody welcome" gatherings. They might include barbecues, a party, or shared community projects. Through these inclusive events, those outside the group can begin the process of making their way into an ethical community.

Pegging with purity: Walking the labyrinth

At the same time, the notion of spiritual tourism reminds us that we need to allow space for people to peg. This is an essential part of being a tour guide. So while the hope is that tourists will eventually move into ethical communities, we must recognize that they may need to enter such communities via the peg community.

surfing in cyberspace: an online labyrinth is available at www.labyrinth.co.uk

Walking the labyrinth is a pure form of peg community. The labyrinth is a purposeful circular path in which the participant moves from the edge to the center and out again. Walking it can be a tool for meditation and prayer. It has the advantage of accessibility, requiring no prior knowledge of church liturgy or religious practice. Equally, it can be laid out with various stations where people can engage with some dimension of the Christian journey at their own pace. However, walking the labyrinth remains a purely peg experience. While you might meet other people walking the labyrinth, or later share your experience with another labyrinth walker, there is no expectation of long-term commitment.

Weaving together redemptive portals with the insights of spiritual tourism can allow the range of expressions of the emerging church to be more intentionally missiological. The house church can ask, "How can we create spaces and places for people to move into our ethical community?" The labyrinth designer can ask, "How can we create stepping stones for people to move from pegging to the ethical dimensions of serving others by contributing to events like the labyrinth?" Both peg and ethical communities are essential to our missiology and the bridges across which postmodern tourists can walk.

Pegging the ethical: The art collective

Alternative worship communities were an early prototype of the emerging church. In the United Kingdom and New Zealand, alternative worship shared the same values of postmodern cultural engagement through the use of image, imagination, and ritual. However, the underlying shape of the community developed into two distinct shapes—I call them the *alternative worship art collective model* and the *alternative worship weekly participatory community model*. Both models offer different ways of mixing peg and ethical communities, and in so doing, generate different missionary challenges.

The *art collective,* as one form of alternative worship community, typically manifests as a monthly (perhaps more often, perhaps less), visually creative feast. Groups—such as Grace in London, Visions in York, or Parallel Universe in New Zealand—that evolved this way were guided by the dream of offering an incarnational expression of worship among a postmodern generation. For communities like these, the art collective is meant to be like a nightclub, with God as DJ. Such an incarnation requires large amounts of time to manipulate video, provide slide images, and create new liturgy and music.

The visuals, music, and worship stations invite the access of a classic peg community. Amid the screens

clubbing: The "nightclub" metaphor for worship is rather frightening. I know you are not advocating this image. But it is an image that captures modern alternative worship. Basically, as I understand it, the nightclub is a dazzling show. I have watched worship "programmers" (a modern term) create worship experiences (another modern idea) for people who watch and listen (the consumer). The burnout rate of this so-called worship is very high. But more importantly, worship is not a program done to us or for us. Worship is done at God's initiative so that we enter into an interactive relationship with God and God's mission to rescue the world through Jesus Christ. The nightclub image of "to and for" must be replaced by a more biblical image of "interaction and relationship."
—Robert Webber

and samples, individuals share an experience. The very act of watching screens naturally encourages passivity. As with meeting people at a rock concert, engagement with people at such a gathering feels artificial. The small talk revolves around the shared peg experience.

I attended an alternative worship service in the UK on Trinity Sunday, 2001. Participants were asked to make friendship bracelets by weaving three threads together into a bracelet to remind them of the triune God. It was a superb example of takeaway spirituality, a pause in which participants might weave the textures of the worship experience into their lives. Yet this act of worship remained essentially individualistic. We were individual "pegs" making individual bracelets, to sustain our individual spirituality in the week ahead.

There was no shared commitment, no potential engagement as an ethical community. This could have been introduced with the announcement that one of the three threads was a person in this alternative community, or the suggestion that the bracelet be ritually tied by another member as a way of joining us to one another.

My intention is not to criticize this act of worship. Indeed, much contemporary church worship invites a similar mode of response, as the individual is invited to lose herself in God as a solo act. I am merely highlighting the way worship often lets people peg. In fact, the strength of the art collective model is that it is intended as a means for people to peg, acting as a sort of postmodern seeker service.

Interestingly, using Bauman's notions of contemporary community, alongside the pegging community participating in the creative and visual worship experience there exists a hidden ethical community. Behind the screens and the samples is a team of people forming the worship experience. Behind the art collective model of alternative worship are groups of people who are enjoying sustained spiritual growth as they integrate their Christian faith with their culture. They experience community as they share lives and spirituality. Thus, using Bauman's analysis, the art collective is an ethical community offering a peg community through an incarnational worship experience.

The missiological question, then, is how to help people move from the peg community to the ethical community. To touch the true value of redemptive community one must journey behind the screen. The ethical community needs to be intentional about building bridges, allowing those who come for a peg community to enter into the life of the ethical community—bridges such as a post-event conversation at the local café or pub, or an invitation to design future events. It must ensure these pathways are well lit and that the lives of those in the ethical community are evident embodiments of the body of God.

The ethical peg: Weekly participative communities

Another form of alternative worship could be called the weekly participative community (including examples such as Cityside Baptist Church in New Zealand and Café Church in Sydney). Like the alternative worship as art collective, this form shares a commitment to incarnational worship among a postmodern generation. However, since these communities meet weekly, there is less time to develop video loops or new music. Instead, the focus is on more tactile expressions of creativity. Like the art collective, there is a focus on postmodern incarnation and high levels of ownership and participation, but rather than participation occuring prior to the event, participation is an essential part of the actual experience.

Cityside Baptist in New Zealand has a weekly worship service divided into segments. Each segment—call to worship, sung or meditative worship, prayers, hot text,[94] prayer of confession and words of forgiveness, concerns of the church, prayers for others, benediction—is crafted and presented by a different person. As I've mentioned, segment leaders are encouraged to present their

joining in: What that means for me is that when I'm planning worship I'm planning something where the participation has to be in that hour or so we're meeting together rather than anything before it.
—Interview with UK alternative worship leader, June 2001.

doing God's story:
What is it that we
do when we gather
together to worship
God? Worship is to do
the work of God. That
is, in worship we do
God's story. Worship
does not arise from
within us as something
generated by us.
No, biblical worship
does God's story
through proclamation
and enactment. We
interface, not with
an idea of God as
an abstract notion,
but with the God
who acts in history to
rescue the world. So
worship *remembers*
God's story, and we
enter into God's story
as a present action
in history *anticipating*
its destiny in the new
heavens and the new
earth.
—Robert Webber

tell me: If you do know
of any fully formed
models of festival
spirituality, postmodern
monestaries, or
incarnational missional
communities—or think
you've discovered any
other models—drop
by www.emergentkiwi.
org.nz and let me
know.

particular segment in whatever form, style, medium, and level of creativity they wish. Thus a wide range of participation occurs during the worship.

Like the art collective model, this weekly experience allows spiritual tourists to peg. They can observe the participation. Like talkback TV, they can listen to the public disclosure of the private lives of others. They can share the experience without any expectation of long-term commitment.

Yet the fullness of the experience is enhanced through participation. A church member told me, "Cityside is not something that happens on Sundays. Cityside is like living in this flat with people who are Citysiders, so therefore I'm in church every day. I see them on holiday . . . It's much bigger than Sunday."[95] Thus a deeper and more ethically demanding expression of community is present.

Alternative worship mixes peg and ethical communities in different ways. The alert missionary will be pondering well-lit pathways, wondering how people might transition from peg to ethical communities. We'll explore this more at the end of this postcard.

First, let me explore two more emerging models. Unlike the art collective and the participatory community, these models are largely untested. I see groups dreaming about or even evolving toward these models but am not aware of any emerging church groups that would consider themselves fully formed examples.

Festival spirituality

A future form of the emerging church could evolve into what I term a festival spirituality. Such a model is based in the *festival spirituality* of the Old Testament. Israel was a rural nation that lived primarily in family groups. Three times a year the nation gathered together.[96] These festival times included corporate celebrations, expressions of vitality and joy, the giving of offerings to God, and the welcome and inclusion of those on the fringes (the aliens, the fatherless, and the widows).[97]

This festival spirituality was part of the rhythm of Israel; a mix of family groups and regular large-scale celebrations as people swarmed to Jerusalem. (To apply Bauman, it was a mix of ethical and peg communities.) Enriched by the festival spirituality of gathering and feasting, people then returned to their lives loaded with a sense of being part of something bigger. Festivals offered a set of memories that would sustain their spirituality and their identity until the next festival.

Festival spirituality offers much to a postmodern world. It allows smaller ethical communities to be nourished by the variety and choice of large-scale celebration. It allows those on the fringes—on the outside—of our communities to peg with us and sample our lives. It provides tremendous missionary potential. How easy it would be for tourists to join the pilgrim crowd going to Jerusalem and get caught up in a range of spirituality options—experiential, experimental, or possible existential conversion.

I wonder if the emergent church will see more development of larger scale events. Events like Greenbelt or Spring Harvest in the United Kingdom; Cornerstone Festival, Creation, or Sonshine in the United States; Parachute in New Zealand; and Black Stump in Australia are in many ways festival spirituality. They offer choice and create a set of memories around a large-scale gathered event.

A friend of mine runs Black Stump, Australia's largest festival of Christian music, arts, and teaching. Over the last few years he noted a rising trend as more and more young people indicated on their registration forms that Black Stump was their church. Is this crisis or opportunity? The notion of peg and

rescue: Postmoderns rediscover that God's story is told and acted out throughout the Christian year. Advent, Christmas, Epiphany, Lent, Holy Week, Easter, and Pentecost are occasions to feast to God's rescue story.
—Robert Webber

festivals without walls: Festivals work both ways. The Christian community celebrates in festival and we need to make it easy for folks to join the pilgrimage. It is easier if our Christian festivals are held outside, where there are no walls to cross. Equally, other communities have festival celebrations too. Will Christians be part of these festivals?
—Olive Drane

world party: I agree, the festival is a kind of postmodern pilgrimage site. Here in the UK, Greenbelt Festival is not just a "peg" or event—for many of us it's an annual reunion with people who live miles away from us and whom we only see once a year. The festival has another feature that I think is fantastic—it's one of the best ways for the emerging church to remind ourselves that we are part of the universal church—not just "you in your small corner and I in mine," but a much bigger community. That has both encouraging and disturbing aspects: It stretches us and limits us too. It's very healthy to keep the perspective that we don't just write our own script. We belong to something much bigger than our own little communities.
—Maggi Dawn

a spirituality festival: Rather than weekly church services, could religious life be configured as:

- a regular (every four to six weeks), well-advertised festival? It could offer input, child care, missional art projects, and worship over a day. A potent mix of content, creativity, and being together could also be a good place to "stumble into" the church/group.
- weekly café groups that discuss the input?
- sporadic creative and communal gatherings as other expressions of community (for example, storytelling nights)?
- the routine of corporately praying a type of daily office, from traditional Catholic to Celtic?

festival: It is easy for others to join in festival spirituality. John was leading a mission workshop with church leaders in a venue just off one of the main streets in the center of London. By way of worship, he led them in a circle dance, followed by a line dance. In a line dance, whoever is at the head of the line determines what happens next. After taking the group (all 200 of them) around various parts of the church building, the leader on this occasion went out into the street, and round the block before returning. Everyone was surprised that, though 200 went out, about 230 came back in! It was seven o'clock on a summer evening, the street was crowded with people going for a night out—and they were attracted to join a group dancing and singing along the street. As they settled on the floor inside, the Christian leaders were wondering, "What have we done—and why did we do it?" So were the additional 30 people! Their question then became the mission workshop!

—John and Olive Drane

ethical communities can inform our reflection. Rather than see the festival as the peg community and a local church as the ethical community, is it possible to see the festival and church as both? Could festivals take their role as spiritual providers and discipleship resources seriously, not just during the event, but in the months following? Could the local church take its role as a provider of festivals seriously, giving tourists opportunities to "peg" within the life of a local church?

Smaller groups can plan festivals as well. Graceway once ran a day-long festival called Enliven. It was held on Pentecost Sunday and thus became a festival in honor of the Spirit of God.

Enliven offered a mix of seminars, coffee, and an art project. Seminars were a place for input and discussion on the Spirit in our workplaces and lifestyles. Coffee invited community building. An art project gave an opportunity for creative expression— each person was given a blank metal tile, paint, and aluminum cans. An art teacher gave people encouragement and ideas as they sought to express how the Spirit "enlivened" them in that day. People had the choice to move between thinking, drinking, and creating. The event ended with worship and the bringing of the art project into the corporate life of the community.

It was a large-scale celebration that gave a set of memories to sustain spirituality and identity. It energized our ethical life together. It allowed people to tour, to browse our life. One such tourist spoke to me at the end of the festival. She left her church many years ago, dismayed over its treatment of her children. Enliven allowed her to dip her toe back in. She told us this festival was an important step in her spiritual journey back toward Jesus.

Festival spirituality can bring much to a postmodern world. It offers ethical communities a way to extend variety and choice to pegging tourists. They can join the pilgrim crowd going to Jerusalem and get caught up in a range of spirituality options—experiential, experimental, or possible existential conversion.

Postmodern monasteries

Historically, the monastery developed as a place of prayer, which also played a significant role in preserving knowledge and providing education. Perhaps it is time to birth postmodern monasteries as places of prayer and social justice in our contemporary world.

The Name of the Rose, by Umberto Eco, is a fictional account of monastic life.[98] The book finishes with a burned out monastery, destroyed from within by fire. The texts of the library, collected and copied through centuries, are burned. It is the intellectual, rational reasoning of the main character that ignites the circumstances by which the monastery catches fire and the library is burned. And so the central overarching narratives of text, reason, and religion are reduced—literally—to ash.

It is widely considered a postmodern book in its playful deconstruction of text and its undermining of the central place of reason and religion. However, the plot and the deconstruction of texts, reason, and religion are not my focus here. Rather, I want to focus on the monastic ideal that is the backdrop to *The Name of the Rose*.

In the book, we see a group of people who have given themselves to the rhythms of prayer and a way of working within the grace of God. The work of the monastery is to preserve learning. We read of monks who sit

surfing in cyberspace: For the complete paper, see "A Postmodern Monastery." Steve Taylor, IT I Church I Culture, November 2003. For a download see www. emergentkiwi.org.nz/ archives For communal living, German-style, search for "flatshare berlin" at http://news. independent.co.uk/

for hours in the scriptorium, surrounded by a wonderful library, faithfully copying each text. This is the task of this monastery. It preserves knowledge within the rhythms of prayer. In doing so, it sustains literacy in society.

It is tempting to laugh at this laborious copying of texts. After all, we have our OCR and laser printers and Adobe Acrobat software. Yet I wonder if amid our laughter lies the possibility of a postmodern monastery. What would it mean for a dedicated group of people to seek to pass on knowledge within a rhythm of prayer?

As you ponder this question, come with me to Ireland. In Dublin, you can view *The Book of Kells*. The book emerged during the pinnacle of Celtic monastic life around the year 800. As with *The Name of the Rose*, Celtic monks copied the text. But the monks who worked on *The Book of Kells* mixed text with fine art and evocative images, making it one of the most beautifully illuminated manuscripts in the world. It is a wonderful example of a dedicated group of people combining text with creativity, within the rhythms of prayer, to pass on knowledge.

surfing in cyberspace:
Images from *The Book of Kells* are available for purchase digitally at www.bookofkells.ie Some of the images can be seen at the Celtic Art Library at www.celtdigital.org

Such an effort might seem impossible in our quick-take culture, but consider what happened in October 2003. Two New Zealanders, Steve Davis and Rajneel Singh, filmed their tribute to *The Matrix*. They brought together their creative passion, a cast of amateur actors, and a cheap Sony Handycam. They were a dedicated group of people (one of Bauman's ethical communities) seeking to pass on their creativity.

For a cost of $800 (New Zealand), they produced a 15-minute Web-only film, called *Fanimatrix*. They transformed mid-winter Auckland into a futuristic cityscape, via Adobe software. To quote Rajneel Singh, "We hope people will see it as cheap but not cheesy, because a lot of work went into making it a very authentic film."[99]

Their hopes were realized. Word of mouth via Internet chat resulted in 70,000 downloads in the first five days. The Internet enabled the rapid development of peg community. New Zealand's leading newspaper commented:

The film's early success means it has probably

already enjoyed [in five days] more exposure than even the best-known New Zealand short films can muster through the conventional festival circuit. While the move to digital recording and editing has revolutionized the film industry and allowed "guerrilla" film-makers to produce high-quality, low-cost productions, the Web is increasingly acting as an alternative distribution channel.[100]

So can the emerging church create video loops good enough that 70,000 people will download them for free? With contemporary technologies there is a missional opportunity to provide rapid exposure and dissemination of ideas. The development of a "postmodern monastery" has this missional horizon, the dream of a dedicated group of prayerful people who creatively seek to pass on the texts of Christianity.

Len Sweet points out that the Sunday school movement arose in the eighteenth century in an industrial society.[101] It0 was a society in which few could read. Thus not only did Sunday schools evangelize through Christian education, they also aided the education of illiterate children.

This was enhanced by the end-of-the-year prizes—awards ceremonies and prize books to celebrate achievement. Considering the price of books back in the eighteenth century, this had significant educational benefits. It's been compared to a church handing out computers for perfect attendance today. The eighteenth century Sunday school was giving out expensive resources and enabling children to clamber across their literary divide.

Could the postmodern monastery similarly help people enter into the life of the church by crossing the digital divide? Many emerging churches are using the Internet to bring the church to the masses, to give books to the illiterate as it were. But in using technology, we must be cautious not to focus on cool technology for the sake of being cool. Just as *The Book of Kells* was created not

surfing in cyberspace: For another perspective on devotional, communal, incarnational, and missionary orders, see "Apostolic Orders Among the Poor: A Protestant Missionary Order with Vows of Non-Destitute Poverty," by Viv Grigg at www.urbana.org

only to preserve the text but to honor God with a work of beauty, just as Sunday schools taught Bible stories not only to provide reading skills but spiritual skills, so too must the emerging church use technology as a means to a greater end—an invitation to life with God.

In order to remain spiritual and missional, I would suggest a postmodern monastery be earthed in physical space. While the virtual world might offer an initial peg community, it is essential that there be a physical space for human connection within an ethical community.

As with the ancients, postmodern monks need to develop a rhythm of prayer, a shared daily spirituality that ensures their mission is about more than the neon glow of a screen. A postmodern monastery needs to take shape within a rhythm of appreciating people, creation, and God.

For those emerging churches who see this as their primary mission, my belief is that they will need to build a community of "monks," a group of people with knowledge—not of copying books, but of Web design and filmmaking and graphic design. Some parttime, some sparetime, perhaps even some fulltime. Together, these monks can develop a few commercial projects to fund their lifestyle, such as authentic, low-budget, group creative projects—video downloads for the world. They can invite teenagers from the neighborhood to use the high-tech gear as a way of building relationships, sharing skills, and developing their spirituality.

Postmodern monasteries could offer much to Luhrmann's world. They would exist as ethical communities, which could profoundly shape participants' spiritual development through prayer. Through the use of their technical skills to teach the digitally illiterate, postmodern monks can express the justice of God. By focusing their creativity, they offer the chance to develop quality creative spiritual products—"downloads"— among the pegging world of the Internet. Our contemporary technologies offer the missional opportunity for

contemporary monastics: I agree that we could learn a great deal from the monastic rhythms of life. Ian Bradley's *Colonies of Heaven* (London: Darton, Longman & Todd, 2000) offers some inspiring suggestions about how the features of Celtic monasticism could be readily adapted to a postmodern culture. For the braver ones among us, there is no better way of getting a grip on what that actually means than making a retreat for a week or more in a real live monastery. There's something about monastic spirituality that can't be understood by theorizing, but only by engaging with it on its own terms. Finding out firsthand how and why different forms of monastic life work, puts you in a good place to think through the similarities and differences between the monastery and the postmodern Christian community.
—Maggi Dawn

the creatively gifted to pass on the life-giving texts of Christianity.

Well-lit pathways

In some sense, the church is both a peg community and an ethical community. The love of God demands an ethical discipleship within an ethical community. The love of God offers a place to gently explore that love in a peg community.

Yet each of the emerging church forms outlined here struggles to be both peg and ethical. House churches share deep relationships, but are hard for strangers to enter. Alternative worship, in both its art collective and weekly participatory forms, creates space to peg and offers the spiritually formative planning group, but the pathways from one to the other need to be clearly lit. A festival spirituality can offer both peg and ethical community, and such forms warrant further exploration. A postmodern monastery suggests an ethical community, but will require entrepreneurial skills in order to sustain a peg community.

Spiritual tourism reminds me that tourists are on a pilgrimage. Some are experiential, wanting the space to peg and look for meaning. Others are experimental, weighing the integrity and depth of the body of God. Some will existentially convert and need clear ways to embrace ethical community and the long-term redemptive love offered by the body of God.

No matter the route they take, mission to the spiritual tourist requires well-lit pathways. These include:

- Information, in labels and in leaflets, on how to take the next step.
- Skilled guides, clearly identified, who are willing to give guidance on how to take the next step.

- An informative and interactive website (given that an increasing trend is for pegging people to use the Internet to seek information).
- The intentional development of what Australian church planter Mike Frost calls *proximity space*, the "putting of ourselves in positions where we will bump into and interact with those who do not yet follow Christ. This can include formal projects like cafés or informal joining of sporting clubs, work places, universities, book groups, etc."[102]

At its core, Christianity is the living of a long-term relationship, with ethical standards of justice and righteousness, in God and among the body of Christ. God is the missionary God in whom love is always flowing and who gave his Son for the life of people and planet.

Emerging Church Types	Peg Community	Ethical Community	Some Ideas for Well-lit Pathways
House Church	The use of a home makes this form of community impossible.	Opening a home signals a depth of sharing and intimacy.	Combining with other house churches in a monthly gathering can enhance the missional interface.
Labyrinth	Accessible to many. Offers an individualized experience, no matter how many people are walking the labyrinth with you.	No expectation of shared commitment. However, the group setting up a labyrinth could evolve as an ethical community.	Spiritual direction. Discussions of labyrinth spirituality. Forming a creative community to re-create the labyrinth.
Art Collective	Great place to peg and share an individualized experience of worship.	An inner core who often experience tremendous spiritual growth as they plan and prepare worship. Can suffer from elitism and burnout.	Opportunities to share worship experiences. Planning for future worship by meeting in public places to enhance access.
Weekly Participative Communities	Great place to peg. Offers an individualized experience, listening to the lives of others.	The weekly participative community encourages connections with others, and therefore the possibility of sharing in an ethical community.	Continually offer peggers opportunities to take a segment. Create weekly spaces to share lives. Work hard on making these safe spaces, so peggers are not compromised.
Festival Spirituality	Enjoy the celebrative choice.	The groups coming to the festival could be an ethical community, as could the group setting up the festival.	Provision of spiritual product. Use of Internet to build community.Groups that continue to meet in various cities post-festival.
Postmodern Monasteries	Download the "product" created by the "monks." Participate in workshops or training. Drop in to use the technology.	Tremendous potential for an ethical community that shares creativity, prayer, and the depth of the kingdom.	Plan combined community projects. Use celebrations to mark the end of training and offer next steps.

More books

Ashley Barker, *Collective Witness: A Theology and Praxis for a Missionary Order*. Urban Neighbours of Hope, 2000. (Box 89, Springvale, Victoria 3171, Australia.)

Zygmunt Bauman, *Community: Seeking Safety in an Insecure World*. Cambridge: Polity Press, 2001.

Pete Ward, *Liquid Church*. Peabody, Mass: Hendrickson; Carlisle, UK: Paternoster, 2002.

Hi from Auckland, New Zealand. I went to Cityside today. It is nearly Christmas and there were excellent video loops of Advent candles being lit as I walked in the door.

I grab a coffee and sit on a cushion. A brief welcome and then the Joan Osborne song "One of Us" is played. It's a superb "nearly Christmas" question, "What if God was one of us?"

With the question still ringing in our ears, the worship leader introduces a call and response, mixing spoken words with congregational chanting of bite-sized segments of an ancient creed. Is the emerging church starting to "DJ" worship, sampling and mixing video images, contemporary music, and ancient chants to create fresh forms of worship?

1565N

POST CARD

Postcard 8:
Culture Samplers

I sat in a café reflecting on my conversation with the host of a local radio show. He had started puzzled and finished puzzled.

It was planned as a five-minute interview on the local student station. That in itself was exciting. We were planning a church service reflecting on the spirituality of contemporary musician Moby. To have the interest of the radio station showed we were scratching the culture where it was itching. At some level, there was missional engagement with our society.

But once we started talking, the five-minute interview became ten, which became twenty. Try as he might, the host couldn't pigeonhole us. He expected us to fit his biased view that all Christians are close-minded isolationists who want nothing to do with popular culture. So he was trying to work out why Christians would engage with Moby. He'd heard recent rumors of Moby's sexual experimentation—didn't that make Moby too edgy for us? The host's boxes were steel-tight. Christianity equals morals. So why Moby? Or was this a con, a sweetener, a hook, to get people in the church door?

As I thought through this conversation, I realized I should have told him about spiritual DJs—we were talking about Moby after all. I should have explained how, just as a music DJ samples from other sources to create something new, we were working out a way of thinking about church that involves sampling from the culture to create new understandings of God. I should have told him there are dimensions of Moby—his strong environmental concern, his spiritual seeking—that are consistent with the gospel and well worth sampling as we seek to follow Christ.

surfing in cyberspace:
Go play at
www.artofthemix.org/

Remixing gospel and culture

Gospel and culture lie at the core of the emerging church. Nearly every time I talk about the emerging church or alternative forms of worship, at some point I am asked if we are watering down the gospel. This question grows out of a concern that when the church engages culture, culture will take over. It asks us to make a choice: the gospel or the culture.

sampling: As a community, we have a commitment to engage with, reflect on, participate in, see clearly as not being evil, question, and reframe contemporary culture. So we use—without any apology—contemporary movies, music, experiences.
—Mark Pierson

This is a dualism I struggle with. It makes no sense in the context of the emerging church. It makes no sense in the context of contemporary life. And, as I will argue in this chapter, it makes no sense in the context of the Bible.

The world we live in is inviting us to find fresh ways of thinking about the relationship between gospel and culture. Jesus, the Word become flesh, lived and loved in the midst of his culture. He routinely used the common, the familiar, the cultural to help the gospel connect with those who listened to him. He attended weddings and feasts and festivals and made his presence known in his community. Our contemporary mission, then, is to see Jesus fleshed out in the postmodern neighborhood. The Incarnation of God calls us to sample from God's world. This is the mission reflection that must haunt the emerging church.

The alternative worship scene is a stirring example of what can happen when the church takes this mission seriously. The visuals and graphics I've seen in some churches are stunning: crosses etched in jagged red barbed wire, blocks of ice suspended from the ceiling, black polythene ponds afloat with candles, multiple slide projected images of Christ amid creation. This video "eye candy" offers overwhelming takeaway impressions. In fact, it has been jokingly suggested that to be a true alternative worship group, you need more television screens than people. Jokes and visuals aside, underneath is, I believe, a very biblical and very subtle postmodern response to gospel and culture.

This is the Word made flesh in postmodern culture. It is the embrace of Christ as the image of God (Colossians 1:15). It is not Christ *or* culture, but Christ imaged *in* culture. It is a missional engagement that practices both connective expression through images while allowing subversion and resistance. Let me explain this both culturally and biblically.

DJ-ing gospel and culture

Feel free to skip this section if you are a regular clubber. You already know that basic DJ-ing is using two CD players or two vinyl turntables to mix together one new sound. At its most complex, it is the art of finding samples and selecting and mixing appropriate tunes into one fluid package that connects with the emotions and circumstances of a crowd.

For example, Moby's album, *Play*, is based on music taken from 1930s African-American blues and jazz. Moby separates pieces of music from their original context then sets them in a different musical context, thus creating something new.

The art of being a DJ is this mixing and sampling. The practice of separating a piece of music from its original context and setting it in a different musical context can create a range of new meanings. The sample can reinforce or amplify a message. It can ironically subvert or it can clash with an ideology, opening up new meanings in that juxtaposition.

In 2003, a local televised sports program here in New Zealand featured a male sports presenter sitting in a spa pool. Flanked by two silent, bikini-clad women, he offered his thoughts on current sporting issues. In response, I DJ-ed this well-known image. For a service themed around water, I identified a range of relevant Scripture passages. We shot a video of these Scripture passages being read by a woman, in a deep spa, flanked by two silent men. The aim was to sample from culture in order to amplify the message of Jesus as living water, while subverting the male stereotypes around sport.

looping the loop:
Moby's *Play* is a great example. I bought it as soon as it came out. I was the speaker at a Baptist youth camp in California and I chose to limit all the music for the digital storytelling to this album. I took samples from Moby's individual tracks and made loops out of them to attach to my video. This was a good way of avoiding progression in the music, keeping the lyrics out, and giving me some excellent background sonic wallpaper. This is also a good example of a DJ (Moby) sampling widely from many sources, and the end user (me) taking the sampling process another step forward to co-produce what I really needed. I was making new loops out of Moby's loops, and attaching them to video loops. Pretty loopy, isn't it?
—Andrew Jones

DJ-ing Fatboy Slim:
"The majority of
the stuff I do is still
samples. There's not
much actual playing on
a Fatboy Slim track at
all." See artist's profile
at vintagesynth.org

Christ and culture:
I think Jesus was
ambivalent towards
culture. Jesus
embraced people.
In doing so he met
them in their houses,
their shops, their
places of worship
and entertainment.
When he spoke he
used illustrations
that were familiar.
But I don't think Jesus
had much need to
embrace culture; he
was already a part
of it. He was in the
flow of Judaism,
local town life, a
reasonable trade,
local politics, extended
family, friends,
parties, shopping,
discussions of ideas
and philosophies,
attending celebrations
and functions, raising
villagers from the
dead, etc.
—Cathy Kirkpatrick

When we played the video in worship, the response was amazing. It was a highly connective piece of liturgy and caused a deep engagement with both Scripture and our contemporary culture.

In Postcard 2, I told the story of my hairdresser who shopped at the second-hand clothing store and created new fashion out of what she found there. I used that story to illustrate a basic principle from Michel de Certeau: the idea of *strategies*—the ways organizations organize reality—and *tactics*—what people actually do with these strategies. It's a way of describing how people transform the dominant culture in light of their own interests.

When we apply this principle to DJ-ing, we can see that the tactic of sampling can amplify, change, or clash with the strategies of the dominant order. The DJ is "making do," with the tactic of transforming the strategies of the record company. The sampling metaphor remains consistent with de Certeau's focus not on the cultural material (in this case the music), but on its manipulation by users (in this case DJs) who are not initially its makers. The insertion of a sample can reinforce, can rise and amplify the swing of the rhythm. Or the insertion of a sample can ironically subvert the lyrics and feel of the original music. Finally, the samples might clash, and in that contrast, create new understandings.

This notion of strategies and tactics offers another way of understanding contemporary approaches to the relationship between gospel and culture. It suggests a move beyond notions of either a separation from or an accommodation to contemporary culture. The emerging church is sampling from the two poles of gospel life and cultural resources to offer a creative and distinctively transformed way of being a Christian, being a missionary, being the church in Luhrmann's world. The visuals and graphics of an alternative worship service, the ancient and future mixing of chant and video are a distinctively Christian sampling of culture.

The textures of the text

While the idea of sampling music might be relatively new, I find evidence that Christians have been DJ-ing the culture for centuries. A close reading of 1 Peter, and in particular his application of family ethics, suggests that Peter is an early DJ, sampling from culture and from the way of Jesus. At times Peter is remixing to amplify, at times to subvert, and at times to juxtapose, all in an effort to sustain the faith of this exilic community who are now "God's people."

Read 1 Peter 3:1-7:

> Wives, in the same way be submissive to your husbands so that, if any of them do not believe the word, they may be won over without words by the behavior of their wives, when they see the purity and reverence of your lives. Your beauty should not come from outward adornment, such as braided hair and the wearing of gold jewelry and fine clothes. Instead, it should be that of your inner self, the unfading beauty of a gentle and quiet spirit, which is of great worth in God's sight. For this is the way the holy women of the past who put their hope in God used to make themselves beautiful. They were submissive to their own husbands, like Sarah, who obeyed Abraham and called him her master. You are her daughters if you do what is right and do not give way to fear. Husbands, in the same way be considerate as you live with your wives, and treat them with respect as the weaker partner and as heirs with you of the gracious gift of life, so that nothing will hinder your prayers.

In early Greek culture, when you talked about how to be married or how to work, how to parent or how to treat employers, you used a style of literature called "household codes." It was a highly stylized and very well-known way of talking about societal behaviors. The

I wonder if our fascination with sampling from the past is partly due to our recent dismissal of the past during modernity's infatuation with progress and the future. It does seem that the past is the new future. Sampling honors the past, and it situates us in closer community with other artists, both current and historical. To sample is to belong. To sample is to find oneself suddenly located in time and space and, mysteriously, connected to other voices, sounds, and images that are emerging around the same issues. Sampling is not a cop out. It is an act of posterity, and a commitment to community.
—Andrew Jones.

surfing in cyber: Cool quote #1: "'Gospel' always involves a way of living in a social environment...." Cool quote #2: "[T]here is no single proper way for Christians to relate to a given culture as a whole. Instead, there are numerous ways of accepting, rejecting, subverting, or transforming various aspects of a culture...."[103]

cultural chorus was very common: Husbands do this. Parents do that. Slave owners do this.

This same pattern appears throughout the New Testament.[104] This suggests that when the New Testament writers wrote about how to live as Christians, they borrowed, or sampled, from this style of literature. Yet Peter subverts the cultural message of this code by using familiar language to say something radically new. Let me show you what I mean by comparing 1 Peter 3:1-7 with the Greek household codes:

Generic Societal (Greek) Household Code	Household Code in 1 Peter
Greek household code talked to men, mentions wives only indirectly.	Bible household codes talked to wives directly.
Greek household code saw women as the property of men.	Bible household codes described women as responsible moral agents who could influence their husbands by their behavior (3:1-2).
Greek household code encouraged one to behave as if society watched behavior.	Bible household codes encouraged one to behave as if God were watching (3:4c).
Greek household code talked to the pater familias, the head of the house.	Bible household codes saw both spouses as "heirs in the gift of life" (3:7).

Now imagine being a woman in the time of 1 Peter. All your life you have heard the Greek cultural chorus. All your life the Greek household codes have positioned you as a second-class citizen. When Peter starts amplifying, you think you are listening to the same old, same old.

Suddenly the tune changes and you are being directly named, "Wives, in the same way . . . ." In Peter's DJ remix, the household code is addressing you. Wives are now amplified and juxtaposed alongside husbands.

Peter's remix continues. Not only are you addressed, you are also a free moral agent with the potential to influence men, "won over without words by your behavior." Women can, with their behavior, influence others. Peter's amplification is now subverting existing cultural norms.

Peter's remix continues. Both partners in marriage are "heirs in the gracious gift of life." There is mutuality in divine relationship. Peter's household codes subvert gender relationships.

Peter is DJ-ing. He took an everyday cultural mix, one of his culture's contemporary singles, and amplified the beat. He has created a new mix, juxtaposing wives alongside husbands and subverting through behaviors and in mutual spiritual relationships. While Peter's words might sound old-fashioned to us, set in his day, in a culture of competing household codes, Peter was very radical. He spoke to women and gave them transformative power. He is almost feminist. He mixed an alternative social ethic in contrast to the beat of society. It is a remix of extraordinary power because it uses the cultural beat to say something new. It mixes gospel and culture in a classic example of "making do," a transformative poaching from, and creative subverting of, everyday practices.

Our world is not Peter's world. Our world is even more sophisticated at mixing and our culture is much more fragmented than Peter's culture. There are so many more samples to use. So many movies create humor by referencing other movies. So much of music remixes old hits and classic bass beats. Nevertheless, 1 Peter shows an early DJ at work. This has

appropriation or contextualization?

It's not about getting stuff from outside to make our worship life more interesting. It's about getting the rubber on the road. About letting what we find out from the Bible rub up against our work life, our home life, our fun, our socializing, our passions, our hobbies, our desires for the future, the last thoughts we have before we go to sleep. While they remain separate, how can we be sanctified?

Don't sample from someone else's life— sample from your own. It's about context—where you live, who you know, your passions, your pains, your yearning for justice, your problems and those of people around you. If you bring these into your worship space, then you may make connections you have never before been able to make, and so take God and his ways with you back into your everyday existence.

It's not about asking: "What works? What's new? What will make us relevant?" It's about asking: "What is my context? Who are the people around me? What are the needs here? Where is God in all this?"

—Cathy Kirkpatrick

a number of implications for gospel and culture in our world today.

Peter understood that we are born into a culture, one with messages, norms, and expectations that we know simply because we live with them every day. We can't ignore them even if we want to. So it makes sense for those who want to bring others into the culture of Christ to recognize and acknowledge the voices of the prevailing culture, its media, its messages, its mores. We cannot live out the gospel of Jesus in the neighborhood if we are unwilling to move in with it.

At the same time, the church needs to DJ distinctly, to take the way society says people should behave, the household codes of our culture, and remix them, humming, changing, subverting, recombining, reinterpreting them. Peter doesn't simply grab what he needs from the culture to make his words relevant. He samples from the gospel and adds his own Christian bass beat. He addresses women and informs them their behavior *can* change their husbands. Peter is speaking words of cultural challenge. Christianity is distinctive. It is transformative. At the heart of DJ-ing is this transformative "making do."

Peter as a DJ asks us to move away from Christian cultural isolation and beyond cultural accommodation. Some bits of our culture we will amplify and applaud, other bits we will sample to subvert and juxtapose. As we see in 1 Peter, neither isolation (the tendency of conservative Christianity) nor accommodation (the tendency of liberal Christianity) is the answer. It is the willingness to remix the culture that will allow us to be the missional church we are called to be.

DJ-ing worship: an introductory (Advent) liturgy

As part of my research on the emerging church, I participated in a DJ mix of song, video, and Christian chant at an Advent[105] service at Cityside Baptist in Auckland. It is a fine example of a contemporary worship DJ in action. Let me take you there.

salt and light: "Let me tell you why you are here. You're here to be salt-seasoning that brings out the God-flavors of this earth. If you lose your saltiness, how will people taste godliness? You've lost your usefulness and will end up in the garbage.

Here's another way to put it: You're here to be light, bringing out the God-colors in the world. God is not a secret to be kept. We're going public with this, as public as a city on a hill. If I make you light-bearers, you don't think I'm going to hide you under a bucket, do you? I'm putting you on a light stand. Now that I've put you there on a hilltop, on a light stand—shine! Keep open house; be generous with your lives."

—Matthew 5:13-17, from *The Message*

We enter and see that around the room are six television sets. The same video is playing on each—footage of Advent candles being lit. (An ancient liturgical practice is to light a candle for each of the four Sundays of Advent, a symbol of our gathering and growing expectation.) On the video first one candle is lit, then two, then three, then four. Then the video loops back to the start.

visual grace: www.smallfire.org/grace_fire.html

As people settle, another video is inserted and Joan Osborne's "One of Us" is played—

> What if God was one of us
> Just a slob like one of us
> Just a stranger on the bus
> Trying to make his way home?[106]

When the song ends, the worship leader speaks, "In answer to the question [what if God was one of us], God replies, 'I am. I am one of you.'"

Then a chant is introduced, words mixed with a hymn sample.[107]

> Leader: Behind the corridors of space, before the worlds began, beyond all understanding
> . . . God.

> *Congregational chant:* Gloria, Gloria, Gloria, in excelsis!

> Leader: Fathering time, mothering creation, parenting all people
> . . . God.

> *Congregational chant:* Gloria, Gloria, Gloria, in excelsis!

> Leader: Waiting for the right moment, preparing the right way, intending the right woman
> . . . God.

Congregational chant: Gloria, Gloria, Gloria, in excelsis!

Leader: We believe in one God . . .

Congregation: . . . *Maker and mover of heaven and earth.*

After the chant, a member of the congregation walks forward to the Advent wreath. In it sit five candles: a candle for each of the four weeks of Advent, plus a central Christ candle to be lit on Christmas Day. This being the third Sunday of Advent, two candles are already lit. The congregational member holds a lit taper to the third candle on the Advent wreath.

This is DJ-ing worship—a sampling of video, candles being lit, song, affirmation, and chant. The chant samples new words (God as mother, as father) with a line from a traditional hymn (*Gloria in excelsis*) separated (sampled) from its original musical context. A further ancient sample is added from the Nicene Creed ("We believe in one God, Maker . . ."). The traditional hymn and ancient creedal words are remixed with contemporary words.

This becomes an incredibly meaningful moment for me. An ancient creed is suddenly life-giving, providing answers to contemporary cultural questions. Christianity has answers to the pop cultural world I inhabit. The short samples of chant, hymn, and creed not only hold my attention, but they reorient me toward God.

When the worship leader, acting as worship DJ, mixes Joan Osborne and the Christian understanding of Incarnation, we find sampling the perfect tool for creating a new understanding of the gospel. "What if God was one of us?" sneers Joan. "God *is* one of us," is the quiet affirmation of the DJ. The words of the liturgical chant subvert Osborne's notion of God as a stranger on the bus by speaking of God as a companion—fathering, mothering, and parenting.

The use of contemporary video technology to enact the ancient tradition of lighting the Advent candles amplifies the meaning of this ritual. Traditionally,

hints for new DJs: Hunt the liturgical archives (other denominations' prayer books, worship prayers from other countries, art images from other places) looking for word samples. Hunt liturgical history looking for ancient depth. Mix this ancient wisdom with new sounds and images.

the church has seen Advent as a double glance. It is a glance back to the advent of Jesus, the Christ, as helpless babe. And it is a glance forward, anticipating the return of Jesus, the Christ, as triumphant King.

So Advent is about both beginnings gone and endings to come, about glancing forward and back, about one person who appears twice in time. Advent displaces linear notions of time and space. It asks you to look two ways at once and see one person in two time zones. And you thought air travel or reading a New Zealander's Monday blog when it is still Sunday in the United States was weird!

Consider, too, the video sampled at Cityside. A candle is lit so the act is complete. But no, because the sample is looped, there is another beginning. Sampling the looping video, in which the beginning that is already over is followed by another beginning and another, serves to amplify the mystery and wonder of Advent.

Consider also that the act of lighting the Advent candles was filmed and looped before this Sunday worship event. The video loop is then a historical act. Yet alongside the video sample, worship participants also watch the third Advent candle being lit in real time. Again, linear notions of time and space are displaced. Consider finally that the act of lighting candles is an ancient church practice. Yet in the video sampling it is presented in a contemporary manner. Past and present, ancient and contemporary, are remixed. Throughout the service, sampling creates new meaning by taking what is familiar and expected and presenting it in ways that make us take another look, make it unexpected. Suddenly we have a new understanding, a new sense of God's work in the world.

This is not gospel or culture. This is not fundamentalism or assimilation. This is DJ-ing, a distinctive and transformative remixing of both gospel and culture.

God in culture: Behind this lurks the theological affirmation that the Spirit of God is present in the world. Christians follow God in the world, the same God who spoke through a donkey to Balaam in Numbers 22, who acted through a foreign oppressor in Nehemiah 2 and Esther 5. God is present in our culture.

This can be scary terrain. I find it helpful to remind myself of Paul's understanding of the Spirit as the Spirit of Jesus. It is a term unique to Paul.[108] The Spirit is in the world. Yet there are a lot of spirits in the world. The Spirit I am looking for is the Spirit of Jesus, distinctive in the Christian gospels. It is an enculturated remix.

in the DVD player: *1 Giant Leap* is a project by Jamie Catto and Duncan Bridgeman to explore global cultures in a search for deeper unity.[109] A single on the DVD is titled "My Culture [Sketch]." It features images of African villages, a clubbing mirror ball, George Nuku speaking of his Maori ancestors, Kurt Vonnegut speaking of TV as a provider of artificial friends and relatives, Maxi Jazz and Robbie Williams singing, Dennis Hopper discussing the words of Jesus, and Johnny Clegg proudly proclaiming his identity.

As you watch the DVD, note how many cultural influences intersect. You could take a pencil and draw a line for each—African, clubbing, Maori, English, TV. As Christians, we live at the intersection of many cultural influences. It can be overwhelming, unless we take bite-sized pieces.

DJ-ing for mission

Clearly, sampling and remixing has a number of profound implications for mission. Yet it can only be effective if we are conscientious DJs who stay true to Peter's example of using the culture to create something that honors God. Doing so means keeping the following things in mind:

It is unbiblical to be removed from our culture or to ignore the way our culture communicates. The power of 1 Peter is the use of the chorus lines of the culture. Heads nod. Feet tap. This immersion is consistent with the rest of 1 Peter. When Peter calls his community strangers in the world (1 Peter 1:1), he is drawing from the Jewish exile tradition in which the scattered people of God embraced their cultural world, planting gardens, buying houses, consuming goods and services (Jeremiah 29:5-7).

Remix live. Bring a pile of local newspapers to your worship service. Offer coffee and muffins and invite people to read the newspapers. Invite guests who can share a Christian perspective on the news—local, national, international. Place stations around the room for praise, intercession, and offering. Invite people to rip out relevant articles and place them on the various stations as acts of response to the Spirit at work in our culture.

It is also unbiblical to be the same as the culture. The power of Peter's text is that he subverts the chorus lines of the culture. The exiled people of God are to live distinctly among the gardens and houses of the culture. In the Incarnation, God redeems culture. Jesus stands as a reminder that this act of incarnation is no assimilation or acquiescence to culture. The embrace of culture is an act of transformation. It is a distinctive remix.

Remix live. Do a worship series called "Don't sit too close to the TV." Have a fun quiz to find the most TV-tuned members of your community. Have conversations about how to watch TV through a redemptive Christian perspective.

DJ-ing means that culture becomes more bite-sized. Modernity urged one overarching way of seeing the world—that of that one, British male voice in Zeffarelli's *Romeo and Juliet*. But in Luhrmann's *Romeo and Juliet*, flashing images and text and the female black announcer remind us that in postmodernity, culture fragments. It is not one emerging culture, but many emerging cultures.

It was Jean Francis Lyotard who named our culture postmodern.[110] He wrote of society as a complex and mobile "fabric of relations." DJ sampling allows incarnational living at the fluid intersections of Luhrmann's world. Theologian Miroslav Volf notes that, "Christian difference is always a complex and flexible network of small and large refusals, divergences, subversions, and more or less radical alternative proposals, surrounded by the acceptance of many cultural givens. There is no single correct way to relate to a given culture as a whole, or even to its dominant thrust; there are only numerous ways of accepting, transforming, or replacing various aspects of a given culture from within."[111]

The relationship between gospel and culture is one of plurality, bite-sized sampling from everyday life. The image of DJ-ing provides a way to access this bite-sized culture. That entails sampling the concrete practices of the buying of houses and cars; the selections of film, video, and music; the offering of hospitality and friendship. We are called to take life one sample at a time, remixing the fragments of what it means to live ethically.

Peter the DJ invites us to drop our modern dreams of conquering the master narratives. Volf says, "Christians have no place from which to transform *the whole culture they inhabit*—no place from which to undertake that eminently modern project of restructuring the whole social and intellectual life, no virgin soil on which to start building a new, radically different city . . . all transformations are piecemeal transformations of some elements."[112] All we have are the fragments. All we have is trust that in Christ and through the Spirit, these will be enough.

For those at the center and for the preacher in front of a listening crowd, this might seem absurd. But for the missionary looking at a fragmented contemporary culture, this is reality. This is not a denial of the all-encompassing Christ, but a humble acknowledgement that all of our human attempts are just that—merely human. It is a willingness to acknowledge that God is the metanarrative, a grand story so big that all we will ever have is a limited piece of the puzzle. This is a faith affirmation that only Christ and the Spirit can transform our culture.

It is because "Jesus Christ is the same yesterday and today and forever" (Hebrews 13:8), because Christian faith is for all times and all places, that our theologies need to be nonsystemic, contextual, and flexible.[113] Ours is not the task of finding a complete story. Ours is the task of funding, of facing mission one sample at a time.

Remix live. Get into groups during the worship time. Name one distinctive way Christians—

- could treat their neighbors.
- could buy a car.
- could buy a house.
- could manage their finances.
- could make life or career decisions.
- could watch TV.

DJ-ing allows multiple responses along the everyday edges of our lives. Peter DJ-ed among everyday household life, relationships around the dinner table, and over the kitchen sink. Culture becomes not elite books and movies, but the practices of normal life. Or as theologian Kathryn Tanner notes, "What establishes the distinctive identities of cultures is the way in which common elements are used, how they are handled and transformed. What is important for cultural identity is the novel way cultural elements from elsewhere are now put to work, by means of such complex and ad hoc relational processes as resistance, appropriation, subversion, and compromise."[114]

The DJ image allows us to focus on culture as it affects our lives. It allows us to focus on the edges, the interface between gospel and culture, our responses to sexist advertising or local environmental initiatives.

Peter's church was small. Widespread societal influence was beyond it. This did not mean Peter withdrew. Rather he focused on the everyday actions and challenged existing cultural behaviors.

Peter offers us the hope that, no matter what our spheres of influence, we can offer a new gospel mix if we focus on our everyday interactions. As I explored in Postcard 2, it is at the edges of culture, the intersections, on the boundary lines, that the most fertile and provocative missional mixes will occur.[115] It is time to DJ an edgy everyday cultural remix.

Remix live. Our church community ran the "Thinking Room" (this was the notorious "Moby" event I mentioned earlier). We brought in sofas and included everyday cultural items, including contemporary music and poetry. As we worked the edges of our everyday culture—sampling Moby, DJ-ing the ethics of his sexuality and spirituality—the radio station called. Our difference as a community had become evident, giving us radio play, widening our sphere of influence.

DJs can never forget their relationship with the community. In Pacific Island hip-hop, the crowd applauds with hands raised, middle finger and thumb forming a circle and the remaining fingers pointing toward the DJ. This is a feedback loop. It is a non-verbal "amen." The community provides

overlap: In thinking of spirituality, some common elements are surely God's story (the mission Dei, God at work in the world), the Bible stories (of the faith of people and nations), and our own personal stories (the experimental living of the Christian life). Draw them like a Venn diagram, and maybe the high point where they overlap is the place where a good DJ sees, hears, and senses lift off and responds.
—John and Olive Drane

icons: Icons in church? Organs in church? Overhead projectors in church? Video projectors in church? Singing in church? Jazz and soul music in church? Healing in church? Drums in church? Heaters in church? Children in church? Electric lights in church? Street people in church? Bibles in church? English in church? Alcohol in church? Gentiles in church? Dancing in church? Talking in church? Pets in church? Fun in church? Silence in church? Women in church? Amplification in church? Tongues in church? Applause in church? Hats in church? Flowers in church? Homosexuals in church? Paintings in church? Refugees in church? Hymn books in church? Skits in church? Coffee in church? Laughing in church? Spontaneity in church?
—Cathy Kirkpatrick

instant and direct feedback. If the tunes are bad, the clubbers stop dancing and find something else to do. The smart DJ pays attention to the dancing crowd and adjusts accordingly. Effective DJ-ing means allowing our church communities to give us feedback on how well we DJ and on how true we are to gospel and culture.

Thus DJ-ing is an act under communal authority. Peter writes to a church community, DJ-ing with their cultural world. Creativity and play must resonate with the community. For where two or three are gathered, there is Jesus.

Hence his cultural mix is read and played within the church community. Peter as DJ remixed, attentive to the community in which Jesus was present. And because it resonated with that community, because it was affirmed as authoritative and inspired, the mix was handed on to future generations.

It is interesting that in contemporary culture, the DJ-ing community gives and receives authenticity. DJs can go mainstream as long as they remain authentic to their original clubbing community. Sociologist Sara Thornton explains what makes a club—and therefore a DJ—a successful creator of community. She says, "Authenticity is arguably the most important value ascribed to popular music . . . Music is perceived as authentic when it rings true or feels real, when it has credibility and comes across as genuine. In an age of endless representations and global mediation, the experience of musical authenticity is perceived as a cure both for alienation (because it offers feelings of community) and dissimulation (because it extends a sense of the really 'real')."[116]

This is a communal remix, in which community is used to affirm the journey. Our efforts to DJ the culture must be communal acts.

Remix live. Each Tuesday the theme for the Sunday service at Graceway is e-mailed to anyone in the community who is interested. The e-mail might be an image, a Scripture passage, a quote, or a question. People are invited to e-mail back and forth and explore the implications of the theme as a community. This allows the worship leader to DJ in community.

DJ-ing is a learned skill, one that requires practice. The DJ needs to search old record shops, looking for rare labels. She needs to pay attention to sound bites and the messages of her community. She needs ears to hear and eyes to see. These are like the skills of exegesis. As DJs, we must become adept at appreciating the unique contours of biblical literature, at accessing the resources of other church communities throughout history.

The DJ needs to learn what makes the community dance. These are the skills of pastoral listening so that the right track is playing. These are the skills of seeing the world around us, reading the issues, hearing the rhythm of the heartbeats.

The power of Peter's DJ mix is that he learned the household codes of his world. He sat with the Christian story and learned to apply it to everyday lives. He wrote with an awareness of the Old Testament roots. The power of his mix emerged from the interaction between these diverse areas of learning.

This is the role of the pastoral leader in a postmodern world. She leads by example, remixing gospel and culture so that people dance to God's beat. She teaches the community members to DJ for themselves, to handle text and culture in their work places and social spheres. She gives feedback, nurturing young DJs and extending experienced DJs.

Remix live. I dream of seminaries as DJ schools, culturally engaged centers of remixing. Their role is to teach DJs to DJ, and to teach DJs to teach others to do the same. In the meantime, I suggest we invite people to a night of brainstorming ideas for sampling from the culture. Invite a DJ to model the art and ask people to bring in a video clip, a piece of music, a poem, or an art image that has served to amplify or juxtapose an element of faith for them. Encourage one another to become faithful DJs of the gospel and the culture.

DJs should sample with authenticity. When asked about the ethics of sampling from African-American

sampling of Groove Armada: "It was totally by chance. [Groove Armada] was in the countryside recording, and . . . went down to the local shop to buy some food for the night and sitting in this bargain basement bin was this Best of the Fifties hits CD. [They] bought it and fell in love with that [Patti Page sample for {Groove Armada single}, 'At The River']. It has that wonderful '50s chord progression, which is still quite lovely to the ear."
—from www.harmony-central.com

music, Moby replied that he hadn't considered the ethics until his *Play* album was finished.[117] As Christians we need to consider the ethical implications of our sampling a whole lot earlier than Moby did.

The ethnic and the edge are sexy. The danger is that the indigenous is exploited for the pleasure of Western culture. The Body Shop might benefit from exotic products, but what is the impact of this sampling on indigenous communities?[116]

At Graceway, we often sample TV commercials. Authenticity means we try to contact the companies to seek permission for using the commercial rather than taking them straight from the television. Authenticity means we explain to them how we want to use their commercial. (Such a conversation usually involves some bemused questions and becomes a missional conversation in itself!) Authenticity means we don't twist the commercial to reflect negatively on the commercial. Instead we take the meaning of the commercial and seek to add deeper spiritual significance.

I would suggest that the criteria of authenticity be applied to emerging church sampling. We are dealing with someone's creative product. Just as we must sample authentically within our community, so we must sample with an awareness of the authenticity of other communities. We must take time to learn their stories and what has shaped their riches. This will only enhance our sampling.

Remix live. The ethical question I ask myself when I DJ is, "How would I feel if the original author of this sample was present today?" This question keeps me ethically honest. Whether I am using Scripture or Moby, ancient liturgy or U2, am I DJ-ing with sensitivity to the thoughts and setting of the original sample?

Modernity has cast a long shadow over the emerging church. Withdrawal and assimilation have hampered mission and stunted spiritual formation. But when I talk about DJ-ing in the emerging church, eyes sparkle and heads nod. Remixing allows a distinctive missional connection within the culture. Vital spiritual

searching for Tama: It was a mixed class that included a number from non-Western, indigenous cultures including Maori, Pacific Island, and Asian. The young lecturer (me), Western in genetic code and education, but non-Western in birthplace and childhood, introduced the DJ-ing image. Would the DJ image resonate in non-Western cultures? A Maori student wrote an assignment, applying DJ-ing to the search of Tama, an alienated urban Maori, and arguing that DJ-ing would be essential to his finding of identity.
—Church and Society, University of Auckland, Summer of 2004.

growth occurs as gospel and culture, song and Scripture are remixed. The borderlines become a catalyst for emerging life. The community is freed to be who it is meant to be, the authentic body of Christ.

More books

Sarah Thornton, *Club Cultures: Music, Media, and Subcultural Capital.* Cambridge, UK: Polity Press, 1995.

Kathryn Tanner, *Theories of Culture: A New Agenda for Theology.* Minneapolis, Minn.: Fortress Press, 1997.

press play: How to start DJ-ing? Try remixing Moby. Press play:
- on "God Moving over the Face of the Waters" and mix in images of creation.[119]
- on "My Weakness" as people confess their sins.[120]
- on "Run On" as people come forward to receive bread and wine.[121]
- on "We Are All Made of Stars" as people intercede by writing prayers for people in their church community and in their lives on luminous stars.[122]

Part Four
In Advance

Hi. Back home in New Zealand, the postcards became a book. A book is a process in which someone--the author--takes credit for multiple conversations. For these postcards I need to thank:

* Graceway: better friends, better humans, I have yet to find;
* Cityside, Mark Pierson, and many other communities and leaders;
* hu@clara, who opened a closed door;
* the editing pencils of Ian Kennedy, Kelli Robson, Karen Ward, Maggi Dawn, Paul Fromont, Richard Burley, Janette Busch, Simon Smith, and Carla Barnhill.
(The many failings remain mine); and Shannon, Kayli Anne, and Lynne for the gifts of space and love.

I have run out of postcards about the emerging church. How about you write the next ones?

POST CARD

Postcard 9:
Keep The Homefires Burning

From New Zealand and the United States, from the cafés in Seattle and Sydney, from Edinburgh to England, from the cushions of Cityside in Auckland and the bean bags of Visions in York, I have sent you postcards from the emerging church. While Christianity in the West is in decline, new approaches to creativity, community, and ritual are being practiced all over the world. God is surfing the postmodern mission edges of our culture.

This book is my attempt to articulate a postmodern missiology that will be meaningful in a world of increased fragmentation. As we witness the decline of institutions and the rise of tribal community, seeker spirituality, and a fascination with the ethnic and the edge, the church has little choice but to respond with a new mission and a new message.

The emerging church is birthed in Luhrmann's world, in the fault lines of a widespread cultural shift. As it emerges, it represents an attempt at a contemporary, postmodern missiology. Rather than move from theory to practice, the emerging church has simply practiced, sometimes without much theory. The emerging church needs the space to keep practicing, yet it also needs to be theological about its practices. We need to move from emerging by being all about candles to emerging by being a truly new kind of life with God.

Both this book and the emerging church are in draft form. Our contemporary cultural shift is too great to write in any other way. It took my children a number of months to walk and even longer to learn to talk. An anxious parent, I was assured this was normal.

The emerging church is a toddler. This book is written in the hope of encouraging a firmer stride. It is written in the hope of correcting some of the to-be-expected wobbles. It is written in the hope that more

I have sent plenty of postcards in my time: the world distilled down to 105 x 148mm. Just a few lines to say, "I am thinking of you, I care, I am alive, I am experiencing things." Pages to say, "I miss you, I am changing, I can barely describe what I see and feel." But receiving a postcard, however beautiful and nicely written, isn't the same thing as taking the journey; in the same way that watching soap operas is different from having relationships, and reading cook books is different from preparing and enjoying meals. At best they may inspire us, push us a little closer to the edge, encourage us to make our own journeys.
—Cathy Kirkpatrick

words will be written, refining what is, catalyzing what is not yet.

We sit at the fault lines of a cultural shift. We live in a technologically united and fragmented world. Ours is the task of being Christians today and of following Jesus into the future. We can't go back. We can't delegate. All we can do is be responsive to the wind of God in our culture. And that wind of God is inviting us to playfully birth redemptive communities of Christian faith that will confidently DJ, extending spiritual tourism to Luhrmann's world.

All we have is faith, hope, and love. And the greatest of these is love.

Having made my point, it seems appropriate to end a book on postmodern missiology with a story.

Keep the home fires burning

I was speaking at a conference. The punters included two bikers, complete with black leather jackets and black helmets. They sat there all weekend, looking serious.

The conference finished and people came up to say thanks. The bikers walked by, nodded in appreciation, and walked through the door. Then one of them poked his head back in and looked at me. "Hey, have you heard the story about the outback fire in Australia?"

I shook my head. He then proceeded to tell me the story of a tourist traveling through the outback of Australia. For mile upon mile the tourist saw nothing but plain, swallowed nothing but dust. This is the Nullabor. The horizon is deserted.

Suddenly the tourist came across a store in the middle of nowhere. The tourist stopped, engulfed by the silence of the outdoors. Slowly, he pushed his way through the door.

A shopkeeper stood up and asked the tourist where he was from. The tourist shrugged, "Just a tourist."

"Ah," said the shopkeeper. "You are part of the fire. Come on out back." And he pointed at the door.

Puzzled, the tourist followed the shopkeeper out

back. Behind the shop, a group of people, other tourists from all over the world, were sitting around a fire telling stories.

The tourist stopped, stunned by the presence of a fire and a group of people in the middle of the silence of the outback. "This," said the shopkeeper pointing, "is the home fire. It was a gift from a New Zealand traveler. It is called *ahi kaa*, a New Zealand word for home fire. This home fire has been burning for 30 years. From the day the fire was first lit, there have always been travelers gathered around it, yarning, sharing their pilgrim tales. Sometimes there are only a few. Other times there is a whole crowd. And people come from all over the world, gathering to keep warm and share their stories."

Ahi kaa. In Maori the phrase means "to keep the home fires burning." It indicates continuous occupation of land by a tribe or family.[123]

To the emerging church, I say in Maori, *"Kia mura tonu nga ahi kaa mo te matemateaone."*

Keep the home fires burning, so loved ones will always return.

Endnotes

[1] Lyrics from "Longtime," *One Drop East*, Salmonella Dub, Virgin Records, 2003. My transcription of their lyrics. www.salmonelladub.com

[2] This is based on sound bites during Presidential elections. Mitchell Stephens, *The Rise of the Image, the Fall of the Word*. New York, Oxford: Oxford University Press, 1998, p. 139. Citing Center for Media and Public Affairs, Washington D.C.

[3] Jean-François Lyotard, *The Postmodern Condition: A Report of Knowledge*. Trans. Geoff Bennington and Brian Massumi, Minneapolis, Minn.: University of Minnesota Press, 1984, xxiv.

[4] Michel Foucault, *Power/Knowledge: Selected Interviews and Other Writings 1972-1977*. Trans. Colin Gordon et al. New York: Pantheon Press, 1980, p. 131.

[5] Jacques Derrida, "Des Tours De Babel," *Semeia* 54 1992, p. 23.

[6] Ibid., p. 7.

[7] See Kevin J. Vanhoozer, *Is There a Meaning in This Text? The Bible, the Reader, and the Morality of Literary Knowledge*. Grand Rapids, Mich.: Zondervan, 1998. Also Catherine Pickstock, *After Writing: On the Liturgical Consummation of Philosophy*. Oxford, UK; Malden, Mass.: Blackwell Publishers, 1997.

[8] Kevin J. Vanhoozer, *Is There a Meaning in This Text? The Bible, the Reader, and the Morality of Literary Knowledge*. Grand Rapids, Mich.: Zondervan, 1998.

[9] Douglas Coupland, *Girlfriend in a Coma*. London: Flamingo, 1998.

[10] Douglas Coupland, *Polaroids from the Dead*, 1st ed. New York, N.Y.: Regan Books, 1996.

[11] Angela McRobbie, *Postmodernism and Popular Culture*. London; New York: Routledge, 1994, p. 23.

[12] Madan Sarup and Tasneem Raja, *Identity, Culture and the Postmodern World*. Edinburgh: Edinburgh University Press, 1996, pp. 3, 11.

[13] David Lyon, *Postmodernity*. Buckingham: Open University Press, 1994, p. 61. He writes further of the "need to construct our self (image) through the acquisition of the distinctive and different." Lyon, p. 66.

[14] Anna Nussbaum, Letter to the Editor, *Harper's*, October 2000, p. 98. Cited in Tom Beaudoin, *After Purity: Contesting Theocapitalism*. Available from www.ptsem.edu/iym/downloads/lectures_01/AFTERPUR.PDF.

[15] B. Joseph Pine and James H. Gilmore, *The Experience Economy: Work Is Theatre and Every Business a Stage*. Boston: Harvard Business School Press, 1999.

[16] Douglas Coupland, *Life after God*. New York: Pocket Books, 1994, p. 359.

[17] Douglas, Coupland, Generation X. Tales for an Accelerated Culture. 1st ed. New York: St. Martin's Press, 1991, 147.

[18] Bryan S. Turner, "The Possibility of Primitiveness: Towards a Sociology of Body," in *Body Modification*. Ed. Mike Featherstone. London: Sage, 2000, p. 42.

[19] Douglas Coupland, *Generation X: Tales for an Accelerated Culture*. 1st ed. New York: St. Martin's Press, 1991, p. 36.

[20] Ibid., pp. 177-179.

[21] Nelson Mandela, *Long Walk to Freedom*. Great Britain: Abacus, 1995, pp. 699-700.

[22] Peter Corney, "Have You Got the Right Address? Post-Modernism and the Gospel," *Grid*, 1995. Similarly, see also D. Crane, *The Production of Culture*. California: Sage Publications, 1993.

[23] Steve Redhead, *The End of the Century Party: Youth and Pop Towards 2000*. Manchester: Manchester University Press, 1990.

[24] George Ritzer, *The McDonaldization of Society: An Investigation into the Changing Character of Contemporary Social Life*. Newbury Park, Calif.: Pine Forge Press, 1993.

[25] Naomi Klein, *No Logo*. Iberica, Ediociones, S.A.: Paidos Iberica, 2001.

[26] See Roland Robertson, *Globalization: Social Theory and Global Culture*. London: Sage, 1992.

[27] Ziauddin Sardar, *Postmodernism and the Other*, pp. 13-14, 22. It also needs to be noted that the concerns of Sardar are in contrast to the work of Michel de Certeau and his assertion that individuals "make do" in response to popular culture. The notion of "making do" will be discussed in Postcard 2.

[28] See Graham Ward (ed), *The Certeau Reader*. Oxford: Blackwell Pub, 2000.

[29] Michel de Certeau, *The Practice of Everyday Life*. Trans. Steven F. Rendall. Berkeley: University of California Press, 1984.

[30] Michel de Certeau, *Culture in the Plural. Edited and Introduction by Luce Giard*. Trans. Tom Conley. Minneapolis, Minn.: University of Minnesota Press, 1977, p. 49.

[31] The 2004 Stations can be viewed on-line at www.cityside.org.nz/stations/index.html.

[32] Interview with Mark Pierson. Complete interview in Steve Taylor, *A New Way of Being Church: A Case Study Approach to Cityside Baptist Church as Christian Faith "Making Do" in a Postmodern World*, PhD thesis, University of Otago: Dunedin, 2004.

[33] See for example Exodus 12:49; 20:2; or 22:21.

[34] Psalm 137:4, NRSV.

[35] Exodus 31:2-5, RSV.

[36] Bruce Springsteen, "State Trooper," *Nebraska*, 1982.

[37] Certeau, *Culture in the Plural. Edited and Introduction by Luce Giard*, p. 76.

38 "My heart is not proud, O Lord, my eyes are not haughty; I do not concern myself with great matters or things too wonderful for me. But I have stilled and quieted my soul; like a weaned child with its mother, like a weaned child is my soul within me" Psalm 131:1-2.

39 "Can a mother forget the baby at her breast and have no compassion on the child she has borne?" Isaiah 49:15.

40 Isaiah 66:12-13.

41 Further references worth exploring: Isaiah 43:6-7; 44:2,24; 46:3-4.

42 Margaret Hammer notes that the birthing imagery is unmistakable in the Greek and that "Peter's words ring forth as a birth announcement for the messiah and the messianic age." Margaret Hammer, *Giving Birth: Reclaiming Biblical Metaphor for Pastoral Practice*. Westminster/John Knox Press: Lousville, Ky., 1994, p. 64.

43 Terry Veling and Thomas Groome, *Living in the Margins: Intentional Communities and the Art of Interpretation*. New York: Crossroad Publishing, 1996, p. 54.

44 John Drane, *The McDonaldization of the Church: Spirituality, Creativity, and the Future of the Church*. London: Darton, Longman & Todd, 2000, p. 178.

45 Jean-Luc Nancy. *The Inoperative Community*, ed Peter Connor, trans, Peter Conner, et al. Minneapolis, Minn.: Oxford: University of Minnesota Press, 1991, p. 12.

46 Steve Taylor, "A New Generation Leading the Church in a New Millennium," *Reality* 41 2000, pp. 12-18.

47 John Drane, *The McDonaldization of the Church*. Chapter 8 explores midwifery in terms of evangelism. I have taken the metaphor and applied it here to birthing emerging churches.

48 The information that follows is based on an interview with Anne Wilkinson-Hayes of Baptist Union of Victoria in April 2004.

49 Interview with Darren Rowse, April 2004.

[50] Interview with Colin Fletcher, Bishop of Dorchester, United Kingdom, one of mayBe's midwives.

[51] The next five pages are slightly adapted from an article I co-authored with Lynne Taylor, "Choosing Creativity," *Reality* 63 June/July 2004. Used with permission.

[52] Clement of Alexandria, *Proteptique*, as summarized in A. Nocent, "Word and Music in the Liturgy," *Music and the Experience of God.* Ed M. Collins, D. Power and M. Burrim, T & T Clark: Edinburgh, 1989, pp. 128-129. Cited in Banks, pp. 52-53.

[53] Mitchell Stephens, *The Rise of the Image, the Fall of the Word.* New York; Oxford: Oxford University Press, 1998, p. 60ff.

[54] This section is heavily indebted to Robert Banks, *God the Worker: Journeys into the Mind, Heart, and Imagination of God.* Sutherland, New South Wales. Australia: Albatross Books, 1992.

[55] C. S. Lewis, *The Magician's Nephew.* First published in Great Britian by The Bodley Head, 1955. This edition published by Collins: London, 1998, p.114. Penguin, 1955, pp. 93-108.

[56] Banks, *God the Worker*, p. 148.

[57] Banks, *God the Worker*, p. 379.

[58] See also Psalm 66:10; Zechariah 13:9; and Malachi 3:2-3.

[59] See also Jeremiah 10:16; 33:2; 51:19.

[60] See Isaiah 45:9, 64:8; Jeremiah 18:2; and 2 Corinthians 4:7.

[61] For more, see www.moot.uk.net and moot.uk.net/blog/mootblog.htm

[62] See www.godlyplay.com for a full list of resources.

[63] Extract of a poem by Angelus Silesius. Cited and with commentary in Jacques Derrida, "Post-Scriptum: Aporias, Ways and Voice," in *Derrida and Negative*

Theology, ed Harold Coward and Toby Foshay, Albany, N.Y.: State University of New York Press, 1992, p. 313ff.

[64] www.beliefnet.com/story/75/story_7506_1.html

[65] For details of interviews and full quotes, see Steve Taylor, *A New Way of Being Church: A Case Study Approach to Cityside Baptist Church as Christian Faith "Making Do" in a Postmodern World*. PhD thesis, University of Otago, 2004. Italics for emphasis are mine.

[66] *NZ Marketing Magazine*, February 2002, Volume 21, Number 1. The article "Post-Modernist Marketing" on pages 10-18 includes a quiz, "How PoMo R U?" and the presence of postmodernist marketing in six currently running TV commercials.

[67] Christian art images were painted in the catacombs. Eusebius, a historian of the early church, noted the presence of portraits of Jesus. Eusebius, chapter 7, sec 18. Mentioned in Jim Forest, "Through Icons: Word and Image Together," *Beholding the Glory: Incarnation through the Arts*. Ed. Jeremy Begbie, Grand Rapids, Mich.: Baker Books, 2000, p. 84ff.

[68] John of Damascus, *On the Divine Images: Three Apologies against Those who Attack the Divine Images*. Crestwood, N.Y.: St. Vladimer's Seminary Press, 1980, p. 18, Oratio I, p. 8.

[69] Term used by Richard Kearney, *The Wake of Imagination*. London: Routledge, 1988, p. 1.

[70] Kearney, *The Wake of Imagination*, p. 396.

[71] Zizek, "Reading Images," *Reading Images*. Ed. Julia Thomas. Hampshire and New York: Palgrave, 2001.

[72] David Hay, "The Spirituality of the Unchurched," Paper presented at the British and Irish Association of Mission Studies, Birmingham, September 2000, pp. 7, 9.

[73] Erik Cohen, Nachman Ben-Yehuda, and Janet Aviad, "Recentering the World: The Quest for 'Elective' Centers in a Secularized Universe." *The Sociological Review* 35, 2, 1987, pp. 320-345.

[74] "Peace on Earth", *All That You Can't Leave Behind*, U2, Polygram, 2000.

[75] A full order of service is at www.graceway.org.nz/outdoorpeaceservice.htm

[76] B. Joseph Pine II and James H. Gilmore. *The Experience Economy.*

[77] Pine and Gilmore, *The Experience Economy,* p. 42.

[78] Pine and Gilmore, *The Experience Economy,* p. 52.

[79] www.dictionary.com

[80] These are categories used by Cityside Baptist Church in Auckland, New Zealand. www.cityside.org.nz

[81] Bruce also runs the more experimental www.embody.co.uk, which offers an online source of interactive spiritual experiments.

[82] See http://dictionary.reference.com/search?q=redemption and citing Hodge's Systematic Theology. From Easton's 1897 Bible Dictionary: The original data is available from: ftp://ccel.wheaton.edu/ebooks/HTML/e/easton/ebd/.

[83] Douglas Coupland, *Generation X.* p. 8.

[84] Richard W. Flory and Donald E. Miller, *Gen X Religion*, New York: Routledge, 2000, p. 238.

[85] Sharon H. Ringe, *Luke*. Louisville, Ky.: Westminster John Knox Press, 1995, p. 287. "The companion of Cleopas in Luke's story is unnamed, which is a fate suffered particularly by many women throughout history. Given that fact, the travelers may indeed represent another missionary couple in the early church (like Prisca or Priscilla and Aquila, for example)—Cleopas and "Mrs Cleopas," the woman John knows as another Mary."

[86] Johnson notes that the reference to serious heart burn is because "they sensed a conflict of fact, some Latin manuscripts change 'burning' to 'veiled' or 'blinded.'" Thus the focus is not on the heart burn of the preaching, but the heart burn of the struggle to integrate the preaching with their life experience.

Luke Timothy Johnson, *The Gospel of Luke*. Collegeville, Minn.: The Liturgical Press, 1991, p. 397.

[87] "Peasant villagers as a rule, however, tended to be suspicious and mistrustful of strangers, because outsiders often violate the interests of the village community." Douglas E. Oakman, "The Countryside in Luke-Acts." In Jerome H. Neyrey, ed. *The Social World of Luke-Acts: Models for Interpretation*. Peabody, Mass.: Henrickson, 1991, p. 166.

[88] Darrell L. Bock, *Luke*. Downers Grove, Ill.; Leicester, England: InterVarsity Press, 1994, p. 385.

[89] Lesslie Newbigin, *The Gospel in a Pluralist Society*. Grand Rapids, Mich.: Eerdmans, 1989, pp. 222-233.

[90] Thanks to Bob Carlton. Check out at his blog at http://thecorner.typepad.com/bc/

[91] Miroslav Volf, *After Our Likeness: The Church as the Image of the Trinity*. Grand Rapids, Mich.; Cambridge, U.K.: Eerdmans, 1998, p. 129.

[92] Zygmunt Bauman, *Community: Seeking Safety in an Insecure World*. Cambridge: Polity Press, 2000.

[93] Thanks to Paul Fromont for suggesting the reference. Check out his blog at http://prodigal.typepad.com

[94] The "hot text" is a time when an individual reads a Scriptural text that is meaningful to them and explains why it is significant.

[95] Interview with Cityside member in Steve Taylor, *A New Way of Being Church: A Case Study Approach to Cityside Baptist Church as Christian Faith "Making Do" in a Postmodern World*. PhD thesis, University of Otago, 2004.

[96] Deuteronomy 16:16.

[97] Deuteronomy 16:14.

[98] Umberto Eco, *The Name of the Rose*. Trans. William Weaver. London: Secker & Warburg, 1983.

[99] "Viewers rush for net flick." *New Zealand Herald*, 03.10.2003, by Richard Amatatua, www.nzherald.co.nz/storydisplay.cfm?storyID=3526734&thesectio n=technology&thesubsection=general&thesecondsubsection=

[100] Ibid.

[101] Len Sweet, Christchurch, 2001.

[102] www.livingroom.org.au/blog/archives/p_is_for_emerging_missional_church.php

[103] Miroslav Volf, "Soft Difference. Theological Reflections on the Relation between Church and Culture in 1 Peter." *Ex Auditu* 10 (1994), 15-30. Available online at http://www.deepsight.org/articles/volf.htm

[104] Ephesians 5:21-6:9; Colossians 3:18-25; 1 Peter 3:1-7

[105] Advent is the season in the church year in which we prepare for and anticipate the coming of Christ on Christmas Day.

[106] Joan Osborne, "One of Us." *Relish*. Blue Gorilla/Mercury, 1995.

[107] I was later to discover that this was taken from the Iona resources. The Wild Goose Worship Group, *Cloth for the Cradle: Worship Resources and Readings for Advent, Christmas, and Epiphany*. Glasgow: Wild Goose Publications, 1997.

[108] Note for example the term, "Spirit of Christ" in Romans 8:9, "Spirit of God's Son" in Galatians 4:6, and "Spirit of Jesus Christ" in Philippians 1:19.

[109] Duncan Bridgeman and Jamie Cato, *1 Giant Leap*. DVD, Palm Pictures, 2002.

[110] Lyotard, p. 15.

[111] Miroslav Volf, "When Gospel and Culture Intersect: Notes on the Nature of Christian Difference," *Evangelical Review of Theology*, 22, 3, 1998, p. 204. Author's italics have been removed.

[112] Ibid., pp. 204-205.

[113] Miroslav Volf, "Theology, Meaning and Power: A Conversation with

George Lindbeck on Theology and the Nature of Christian Difference," *The Nature of Confession: Evangelicals and Postliberals in Conversation.* Ed. Timothy R. Phillips and Dennis L. Okholm, Downers Grove, Ill.: InterVarsity Press, 1996, p. 65.

[114] Kathryn Tanner, *Theories of Culture: A New Agenda for Theology.* Minneapolis, Minn.: Fortress Press, 1997, pp. 57-58.

[115] "Christian distinctiveness is something that emerges in the very cultural processes occurring at the boundary, processes that construct a distinctive identity for Christian social practices through the distinctive use of cultural materials shared with others." Tanner, *Theories of Culture,* p. 115.

[116] Sarah Thornton, *Club Cultures: Music, Media, and Subcultural Capital.* Cambridge, UK: Polity Press, 1995, p. 26.

[117] Moby said, "It wasn't when I was making the record, but then I finished it and a friend said, 'You might get in trouble for this, people might really have a problem with it.' But my feeling is, I was just approaching it from a naive, genuine perspective." www.disquiet.com/moby.html

[118] For more on this, see Ziaddhun Sardar, *Postmodernism and the Other: The New Imperialism of Western Culture.* Pluto, London, 1998.

[119] Moby, "God Moving over the Face of the Waters," *I Like to Score Vol. 1,* Elektra, 1997.

[120] Moby, "My Weakness," *Play,* Mute Records, 1999.

[121] Moby, "Run On," *Play,* Mute Records, 1999.

[122] Moby, "We Are All Made of Stars," Mute Records, 2002.

[123] Definition sourced from www.courts.govt.nz/maorilandcourt/glossary.htm

emergent
ys

Dan Kimball

the EMERGING church

Vintage Christianity For NEW GENERATIONS

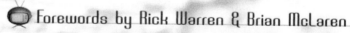
Forewords by Rick Warren & Brian McLaren

WITH COMMENTARY BY: Rick Warren Howard Hendricks
Brian McLaren Sally Morgenthaler Chip Ingram Mark Oestreicher